Prayer for People Who Think Too Much

Prayer for People Who Think Too Much

A Guide to Everyday, Anywhere Prayer from the World's Faith Traditions

Mitch Finley

Walking Together, Finding the Way

SKYLIGHT PATHS Publishing

WOODSTOCK, VERMONT

Prayer for People Who Think Too Much:
A Guide to Everyday, Anywhere Prayer from the World's Faith Traditions

Copyright © 1999 by Mitch Finley

Library of Congress Cataloging-in-Publication Data
Finley, Mitch.
Prayer for people who think too much : a guide to everyday, any-
where prayer from the world's faith traditions / by Mitch Finley.
p.   cm.
Includes bibliographical references (p.   ).
ISBN 1-893361-00-4 (hc)
1. Prayer Comparative studies. 2. Spiritual life. I. Title.
BL560.F565   1999
291.4'3—dc21   99–24027
                                                  CIP

First Edition

10 9 8 7 6 5 4 3 2 1

Manufactured in the United States of America
Jacket design by Drena Fagen
Text design by Sans Serif, Inc.

Walking Together, Finding the Way
Published by SkyLight Paths Publishing
A Division of LongHill Partners, Inc.
Sunset Farm Offices, Route 4
P.O. Box 237
Woodstock, VT 05091
Tel: (802) 457-4000
Fax: (802) 457-4004
www.skylightpaths.com

Contents

Acknowledgments

My thanks to Jon M. Sweeney of SkyLight Paths for inviting me to write this book. Sincere thanks to Arthur J. Magida for valuable editorial assistance.

Preface

WELCOME TO THE QUEST

Books on prayer are not in short supply. Some discuss the theology or philosophy of prayer. Some are collections of prayers. Many teach you how to pray. More than a few offer inspiration and encouragement to help you keep your dedication to prayer alive and kicking. This book is different. This book is for everyone who puzzles over what prayer is, or means, or does. Prayer is not a puzzle to be "figured out." This is the most important message of *Prayer for People Who Think Too Much*.

The second purpose of this book is to help you see prayer from perspectives other than the one you generally take for granted. The innovators of prayer in various faith traditions show us how the *practice* of prayer can change our lives. They will enrich your own understanding of prayer. You will dip into religious and spiritual wells other than your own. Think of yourself as a person who loves home but enjoys visiting other people's homes, too.

This book requires, above all, an open mind. Its purpose is to give you a greater appreciation for the wisdom available from other religions and cultures. This wisdom may help you be a better Jew, Christian, Muslim, Hindu, Buddhist, Unitarian, or whatever you may be—especially when it comes to prayer.

We can learn from each other's experiences and traditions. If you do not believe that, do not read this book. And we can do that without being unfaithful to the tradition in which we are most deeply rooted. Even people who, for the present at least, adhere to no particular religious tradition can benefit from this book, because even so-called secularists have spiritual yearnings, however much they may be poorly defined or acknowledged.

Here are some suggestions for reading this book: read thoughtfully, and open your mind and heart to what other traditions have to offer, then return to your own religious tradition with treasures you would not have found any other way. But don't be satisfied with what you read here. If you find yourself wanting to know more about prayer in Buddhism, Judaism, Eastern Orthodox Christianity, or any of the other traditions discussed here, go to other resources, beginning perhaps with those suggested at the end of this volume. For the more you appreciate what other traditions have to offer, the more you will appreciate your own tradition as well.

On this quest, let your heart be your guide. Follow the thirst in your soul, and your hunger for the divine, for these are behind all desire for prayer.

Introduction

PRAYER IN THE TWENTY-FIRST CENTURY

Listen, now. Here are the brass tacks we need to get down to: Prayer is not supposed to be a "head trip." This book is for people who think too much because most of us live in our head too much of the time. It's true. We may not think of ourselves as great intellectuals, but any time something comes along that we don't understand, our first tactic is to think about it, puzzle over it, try to categorize it, and put it in a cubbyhole.

Take prayer, for example. Too often we think of prayer as a nut that needs to be cracked. For countless people, prayer is a problem to be solved. So they try a prayer or a meditation technique, abandon it, then try another prayer method and soon abandon it, too. We read about prayer, listen to lectures on prayer, watch videos on prayer, and maybe attend retreats on prayer. Maybe, we think, a visiting guru can help solve the problem of prayer. But prayer is not a problem. Prayer is a mystery, and by no means are these the same thing. Not by a country mile.

The twofold purpose of this book is to give a poke in the eye to the "prayer is a problem" syndrome and offer ways to enrich our prayer life and spirituality by learning from the experience and wisdom of various faith traditions. As the author of this book I presume that you, the reader, are actively involved in, or at least curious about, some form of spiritual life. Perhaps you are even active in a religious or spiritual community of some kind. Maybe you are trying to puzzle out the role, if any, of "organized religion" in your life. Regardless, you are curious about prayer and how it might fit into your existence here and now. You are also open-minded about learning about prayer from traditions other than your own.

Before we continue, I want to lay my own cards on the table. I am an active Roman Catholic, and happily so. While this might sound odd, because I am Catholic I consider myself uniquely qualified to write a book that draws on many faith traditions for wisdom and guidance. For the term *Catholic* means "universal" or "all-inclusive," and Catholicism, the religion, is open to whatever is good, true, and beautiful regardless of its source. As a Catholic, in other words, I try to be catholic with a lowercase "c." I try to approach the experience of prayer not just with my head but with my heart as well. I invite you to do the same.

I suggest that we acknowledge that prayer constitutes a mystery. This simply means that when we pray, we intentionally, consciously relate ourselves to God, the Divine Mystery, the Great Cosmic Presence, the Ground of All Being. Whatever. This means we must be willing to live with Someone or Something we will never understand—which is not such a startling remark, since we can say the same for any human being we have ever known, including ourselves. Are you not a mystery to yourself? I thought so.

We must be willing to live with a Nut that will never be cracked. That is to say we will never understand this Mystery with our intellect, but we can understand it in the way that the heart can "understand." We will never crack this Nut with our brain, but we can learn to love It all the same. One of the main benefits of prayer is to learn, through experience, that this Someone/Something is benevolent. Indeed, for at least Judaism, Christianity, and Islam, this Divine Mystery is the Creator God whose "essence," so to speak, is compassion. Prayer helps us to know this with the heart more than with the mind.

MAKING PRAYER MEANINGFUL

To talk about prayer is to address a subject of common human experience. But it is also to highlight a major split in common human experience. Survey after survey, study after study—all reveal that a huge majority of people say that they pray, sometimes often. But let us encounter someone actually praying, and most likely we will act as if we just slipped into an alien world. Take me, for example.

As a writer I was assigned one day to interview the owner of a new restaurant. I knew that this gentleman was from Egypt and a Muslim. Fine. I entered the restaurant, which was beautifully decorated—the walls were painted in warm earth tone colors, the hardwood floors were highly polished, large potted ferns stood in one corner, and the room was filled with beautiful, marble-topped tables and comfortable, contemporary-style chairs.

I approached a young woman who stood behind a counter and asked to see the owner. The employee indicated that he was in the back, in the kitchen. "Good," I said, "he's expecting me." I walked around the counter and pushed open the kitchen door. There was the owner on his knees on a prayer rug, bowing toward Mecca, his head to the floor. He was saying his prayers.

I knew that devout Muslims pray several times a day, no matter where they are or what else they are doing. But I didn't expect to find my interviewee actually *praying*. Knowing that Muslims say their prayers frequently, and stumbling upon a Muslim actually praying on the floor of the kitchen in his restaurant, are two different things. Quickly, I backed out of the kitchen and waited for the restauranteur to finish his prayers. But why was I so uncomfortable upon finding a man at prayer? Why did this startle me so? Why did it unhinge me?

Prayer is a part of my daily life. Perhaps more than the average person, I think of myself as a prayerful person. Unlike most Catholics, but like a sizable minority, I participate in the eucharist, or Mass, almost every day. I believe that God is everywhere, and I believe that the sacred is in the ordinary. I also have earned undergraduate and graduate degrees in religious studies and theology. In spite of all this, my heart skipped a beat when I happened upon a man saying his prayers in the kitchen of his restaurant. I suspect this happened because, like most people in the so-called "developed" Western nations, and even though I sincerely believe in the existence of God and try to practice my religion faithfully, in my everyday life I tend to behave as if God were an abstraction.

In formal religious settings—in church, for example—and in the privacy of my own home and heart, God, the Divine Mystery, is the ultimate reality, the beginning and the end of my existence and the existence of the entire universe: "the Love"—to quote Dante's *Paradiso*—"that moves the sun and the other stars." But in my daily doings, in my work and in my interactions with other people in the wider society, God doesn't figure in the mix even though I sincerely believe this to be so.

In other words, I reflect the dominant secular culture, which compartmentalizes religion, spirituality, and prayer so they seem to be little more than a personal hobby: Whatever you do, warns our culture, don't bring God into "the real world" of everyday life. Otherwise, other people—consumers, clients, fellow employees, what have you—may be offended and start avoiding you. Worse yet, you may be scorned as a religious extremist, a "religious nut case"—and who knows what that could lead to? It could hurt business or your chances for a promotion!

So, we keep our religion, spirituality, and prayers to ourselves, and when we happen upon someone from another culture who does not share the dichotomy we have created between the sacred and the secular, someone kneeling on a rug in the kitchen of his restaurant, we feel embarrassed: Will somebody please tell this benighted individual that there is no God in the kitchen, or at least that he has no business "being religious" in so secular and public a place? Tell him to please go home if he wants to pray?

To put all this in as positive a light as possible, as Protestant theologian Craig M. Gay has written, "contemporary society and culture so emphasize human potential and human agency and the immediate practical exigencies of the here and now, that we are for the most part tempted to go about our daily business in this world without giving God much thought."[1]

This is the context in which we approach the topic of prayer. This is the world in which we live, a world where—except possibly in the privacy of their own subjectivity—people rarely give God much thought. Politicians invoke God at opportune moments—when running for reelection or when there is a natural disaster, for example. But other than that, the Divine Mystery is unwelcome in the world of commerce, technology, and public life. It is important for us to acknowledge that if our discussion of prayer is to be honest, we must be able to discuss ways to enrich our practice of prayer in a society and culture where prayer is, at best, a private matter. All of us might do well to think long and hard about how we plan to fit our understanding and practice of prayer into the society and culture in which we live and breathe.

ONE TRUTH, MANY PATHS

This book will offer reflections on prayer and spirituality from a Western perspective while drawing on wisdom about prayer from other cultures and faith traditions. Be aware, however, that it is not the purpose of this book to encourage the spiritual eclecticism that is so popular today. To say that a Christian or Muslim, for example, can benefit by drawing on wisdom and insights from other faith traditions is not to say that the Christian or Muslim should stop participating in institutional or organized Christianity or Islam and, instead, concoct his or her own eclectic religious and spiritual mix. Rather, *Prayer for People Who Think Too Much* presumes that before you can benefit from other faith traditions, you need to be rooted in *one* tradition and that you plan to remain there. So significant is this point that it is worth listening to the wisdom of three contemporary spiritual masters.

Frederica Mathewes-Green, spiritual mother of the parish at Holy Cross Antiochian Orthodox Mission, Linthicum, Maryland:

> One of the best pieces of spiritual advice I ever received came early, while I was still in college. It was that I should give up the project of assembling my own faith out of the greatest hits of the ages. I encountered this idea while reading Ramakrishna, the 19th-century Hindu mystic. He taught that it was important to respect the integrity of each great path, and said that, for example, when he wanted to explore Christianity, he would take down his images of the Great Mother and substitute images of Jesus and Mary.
>
> We are so indoctrinated by our culture that we can't trust our standards of evaluation. We can only gain wisdom that transcends time by exiting our time and entering upon an ancient path—and accepting it on its own terms. We can only learn by submitting to something

bigger than we are. The faith I was building
out of my prejudices and preconceptions could
never be bigger than I was. I was constructing
a safe, tidy, unsurprising God who could never
transform me, but would only confirm my res-
idence in that familiar bog I called home. I had
to have more than that.[2]

Thomas Keating, a Catholic and a Trappist monk who
lives at St. Benedict's Monastery in Snowmass, Colorado:

The ideal way to develop a practice is to plug
into a tradition that has long-range experience,
literature, and rituals that support it. When
you make a collage of various traditions, you
run the risk of digging too many wells in a
desert, which might take a lot of time, whereas
if you work one well that has a good reputation, where water is to be found, it might be
more rewarding in the long term.

Information about other traditions can com-
plement and enrich your particular path, but
you need to be well rooted before you can derive any true benefit. Without that rootedness,
it's hard to judge the value of complementary
practices, some of which may be peripheral to
the basic thrust of your primary path. Yet with
so many opportunities available, it's hard to
develop the motivation that most traditions require to get to the bottom of what they have to
offer. It may be best to postpone the immediate
gratification of experimentation and invest in
the long-range program. Too much looking
around can be destabilizing. A tree without

deep roots can be blown over by a fairly mild wind.[3]

John Daido Loori Roshi, abbot, Zen Mountain Monastery, Mount Tremper, New York:

> In most cases, hybrid religious paths are a reflection of our cultural trend of greediness and consumerism. With all the possibilities, why give up anything? The consequence of this attitude is that we entertain ourselves with teachings that are meant to transform our lives.[4]

Perhaps Sri Swami Satchidananda, the founder of Integral Yoga Institutes Worldwide, said all this in the most concise manner: "Even though my motto has always been 'Truth is one, paths are many,' I don't recommend trying to walk on all the different paths at once because you will never reach your goal that way."[5]

Ultimately, the spirit of this book was captured by Huston Smith in his modern classic *The World's Religions:*

> What a strange fellowship this is: the God-seekers of every clime, lifting their voices in the most diverse ways imaginable to the God of all people. How does it all sound from above? Like bedlam? Or do the strains blend in strange, ethereal harmony? Does one faith carry the lead, or do the parts share in counterpoint and antiphony where not in full-throated chorus?
>
> We cannot know. All we can do is try to listen carefully and with full attention to each voice in turn as it addresses the divine.[6]

This book invites you to go more deeply into your own faith tradition by learning from traditions other than your own. With that purpose in mind, we will confine our discussion to Judaism, Christianity, Islam, Hinduism, and Buddhism. Since most of us live in secularized Western cultures, in the final chapter we will also discuss how to discover the holy in the ordinary and how that can nourish our prayer life. Keep in mind, however, that the goal is not to put all these insights from several traditions into a spiritual blender but to nourish the roots of our faith tradition, whatever it may be, so those roots can grow deeper and flourish.

Chapter I

Prayer As a Daily Occupation

There is one major obstacle to a balanced understanding of the place of prayer in modern life. This obstacle is the widespread belief in Western secular cultures that if there *is* a Divine Mystery (and many people live as if there is not), then there is still a great chasm between the sacred and the secular, between the holy and the profane. In the United States, for example, the principle of the separation of church and state has been carried way beyond the realm of government. It is now a cultural imperative and a way of life. Most people act as if the sacred had nothing to do with the ordinary, as if spiritual matters were irrelevant to everyday matters.[1]

This attitude exists in virtually all the so-called developed nations today. Work has nothing to do with prayer unless one happens to be a religious professional of some sort: a priest, minister, or rabbi, for example, or a Buddhist monk. If other people are religious, we might think their religion belongs only in formal gatherings of their religious community and in the privacy of home and family life. Bring spirituality into the workplace and you are bound to offend someone. Insert some prayer time into your ordinary, everyday occupation and you will be thought weird or eccentric. Worse, you will be unfashionable. The dominant culture is devoid of the holy, so keep prayer, spirituality, and religion out of it. Hence the inclination, widespread to say the least, to live as if God did not exist. You could even call this attitude, as theologian Craig M. Gay has done, "practical atheism."[2]

> The regression of belief in God, and even more, the decline in the practice of religion, is to the point where from being central to the whole life of Western societies, public and private, this has become sub-cultural, one of many private forms of involvement which some people indulge in.[3]

It is important to acknowledge the reality of this situation, but it is equally important to realize how bizarre and atypical it is when viewed from a historical and global perspective. In the history of the world, no previous society or culture has been so completely devoid of spiritual consciousness as Western societies and cultures are today.[4] It is also true that only in the "developed" nations is this the case, as if technology has so alienated us from ourselves and from the earth that we have also become alienated from the sacred. In such Eastern countries as Thailand and India, entire cultures and societies are based on Buddhism and Hinduism. Everyone takes for granted that prayer is a part of everyday life.

We are in the middle of a vast social and cultural denial of the spiritual roots of human existence. We live our everyday lives as if God did not exist, as if there were no Divine Mystery underpinning our very existence, as if—to quote Dante's *Paradiso*—there were no "Love that moves the sun and the other stars." Instead, we live as if underpinning it all—before birth, during life, and after death—there were nothing at all.

In direct contrast, every major world religion insists that the sacred and the ordinary cannot be divorced. People of faith, of spiritual and religious consciousness, face the challenge of living an authentic spiritual life in a society that grants the freedom to pursue such a life on your own time and in your own place, but denies that life validation in the context of public life and the workaday world. All the religious person can do is cultivate a mentality that is consciously counter-cultural, a mentality that denies the sacred/secular dichotomy most people—even many sincerely religious or spiritual people—take for granted.

Yet, even the most convinced believers in a godless worldview are not without their puzzlements. A prominent contemporary poet and believer in "raising children in a secular way," for example, told of the time his young daughter insisted on attending a church Sunday School. When she came home singing, "Jesus loves me, this I know," the poet squirmed. But he had to admit that he could not tell his daughter that "evolution loves you."

Here is something no one can prove and no one can disprove. The foundation of any fully human way of being-in-the-world is personal experience of the Divine

Mystery simultaneously in and beyond the world—a Mystery that is both immanent and transcendent. This is true no matter where you are, who you are, or what culture you happen to breathe in and out with your every breath. We live in a culture that drives the sacred and the ordinary into opposite corners, and we must decide what we will do about it.

BEGIN RIGHT HERE

God is not, first of all, Someplace Else. Rather, God is radically Here, present and accounted for. Judaism teaches that God is always near. God's primary characteristic is steadfast love: "Be mindful of your mercy, O LORD, and of your steadfast love, for they have been from of old," says the Book of Psalms (25:6).

Christianity defines God in a similar manner. Jesus taught his disciples to call God *abba*, which is Hebrew for "Father." Islam continually repeats its conviction that God is not distant but close. God's compassion and mercy are referred to 192 times in the Qur'an; God is "the Holy, the Peaceful, the Faithful, the Guardian over His servants, the Shelter of the Orphan, the Guide of the erring, the Deliverer from Every Affliction, the Friend of the bereaved, the Consoler of the afflicted . . ."[5]

Although Buddhism and Hinduism often speak in less personal terms, the goals of these religions are similar: peacefulness, liberty, and compassion. The Divine Mystery is just around every corner, under every leaf, shining in everything that is. One of the best expressions of this insight is "Pied Beauty," a poem by Gerard

Manley Hopkins (1844–1889), who was, maybe not surprisingly, a Roman Catholic priest:

> Glory be to God for dappled things—
> For skies of couple-colour as a brinded cow;
> For rose-moles all in stipple upon trout that
>   swim;
> Fresh-firecoal chestnut-falls; finches' wings;
> Landscape plotted and pieced—fold, fallow,
>   and plough;
> And all trades, their gear and tackle and trim.
>
> All things counter, original, spare, strange;
> Whatever is fickle, freckled (who knows how?)
> With swift, slow; sweet, sour; adazzle, dim;
> He fathers-forth whose beauty is past change:
> Praise him.[6]

At the same time, God, or the Divine Mystery, is far beyond and above us and all that we can know or care about. Some would say that God is immanent to the point of transcendence, others that God is transcendent to the point of immanence. Regardless, the point is that the Source and Goal of all being is inescapable and—according to Judaism, Christianity, and Islam—is benevolent. Consequently, the secular/sacred dichotomy, for all its monstrous power to distort people's lives, is completely artificial and a direct contradiction of the truth. Only an implicit cultural atheism can support this dichotomy, and the weird thing about the present state of affairs is that survey after survey reports that the overwhelming majority of Americans claim to be spiritual in one way or another. This can only mean that what supports atheism in the public square is the tacit agreement of all concerned to relegate spirituality to the private sphere and to public occasions where "God" will be spoken of in only the vaguest, often moralizing, terms.

Be that as it may, the person with a spiritual consciousness can strive to live in the knowledge that the dichotomy is false, a widely accepted lie that ultimately has no future. God, as a Christian saint, Augustine of Hippo, declared some fifteen hundred years ago, is closer to us than we are to ourselves, since everything that is, is in the divine. Judaism recognizes God's immanence and transcendence in the many blessing prayers it offers for daily use. When eating: "Blessed are you, O Lord our God, King of the Universe, who makes bread grow from the earth." When dressing: "Blessed are you, O Lord our God, King of the Universe, who gives clothes to cover our bodies." When doing anything for the first time: "Blessed are you, O Lord our God, who has kept us alive until now, so that we may find joy in what has just come to us."

Judaism marks the ordinary events of everyday life with blessings and prayers, and all the important times in a person's life are holy, from birth to death. In addition, Judaism regularly punctuates the year with reminders of important events in history that still have an impact on Jews today, and these are celebrated with religious observances. Thus, history itself is holy.

The ultimate reason for believing that the holy is in the ordinary is directly related to one's image or understanding of the Divine Mystery. In Judaism, God is the Creator whose presence is reflected in creation. Indeed, in Judaism, as in Christianity and Islam, God is personal, not a blind, impersonal "force" of some kind. At the same time, God is not a "person" in the way human beings are persons. Rather, to say that God is "personal" is a kind of metaphor, a way to say that God is "more like a person than like a thing, more like a mind than like a machine."[7] This means that we can relate to the Divine Mystery on everyday, intimate terms, no matter where we are or what we are doing. God is everywhere, and all things are holy. Islam, too, shares a sense of intimacy with God:

> Beginning, as always, with the Qur'an and traditions of Muhammad, Muslims have developed ways of reading and interpreting the sacred sources with an eye for references to God's nearness. In addition, Muslim writers, poets, and artists across the world have evolved dozens of literary and visual forms by which to express their experience of God's presence in everything from communal ritual prayer to glorying in a sunset to the tragedy of heartbreaking loss.[8]

The presence of the holy in the ordinary comes through clearly in the opening words of a prayer that Muhammad recommended to those making a pilgrimage to Mecca: "O God, indeed you know and see where I stand and hear what I say. You know me inside and out; nothing of me is hidden from you."[9]

In Islam, a dichotomy between sacred and secular is completely unacceptable. "In Islam, the Spirit breathes through all that reveals the One and leads to the One, for Islam's ultimate purpose is to reveal the Unity of the Divine Principle and to integrate the world of multiplicity in the light of that Unity. Spirituality in Islam is inseparable from the awareness of the One, of Allah, and a life lived according to His Will."[10]

FINDING THE HOLY
IN THE ORDINARY

To find the holy in the ordinary means, among other things, cultivating an awareness of God's presence, the presence of the Divine Mystery, in any and all situations, no matter how ordinary or mundane. There is no human situation or activity—even those where the Void, or Darkness, or Evil seems predominant—where God's presence is not ready to burst through the instant that human free will opens the door to that presence.

God is present in the daily doings of family life. The sixteenth-century Spanish Catholic mystic and saint Teresa of Avila expressed it as well as anyone—and better than most—when she said that "Christ moves among the pots and pans."[11] The Divine Mystery is not alien to but at home with everything that constitutes the fabric of ordinary human relationships and ordinary human activities. God is in the everyday love of husband and wife when they care for each other in ordinary ways, when they struggle to work through conflict, when they share—to put it quaintly—the pleasures of the marriage bed, and when they strive together to raise their children in a sometimes counterproductive secular culture.

An authentic spirituality resists the dominant culture's divorce of the secular from the sacred, finding that even in such a culture God is present in the people and human activities that fill the average day. Even when the dominant culture restrains people from acting out their faith in overt ways, the authentically religious person perceives the sacred everywhere, even if this makes him or her sometimes feel like a stranger in a strange land.

One of the most important ways to cultivate and maintain a sensitivity to the holy in the ordinary in a secularized culture is through regular prayer and meditation. When the great world religions insist on the importance of prayer and meditation, a living spirituality takes heed, no matter what a person's primary or foundational religious tradition may be. This may take the form of daily reading and praying with sacred scriptures—from whatever tradition—or it may mean giving time each day to a discipline of meditation. Incorporating a prayerful awareness into everyday life may not be as complicated as it sounds, however.

The Russian Orthodox tradition offers a discipline called the Jesus prayer that is specifically intended for use in the midst of everyday concerns and preoccupations. The prayer is discussed in the nineteenth-century Russian classic *The Way of a Pilgrim*.[12] The basic story is simple and charming. The anonymous author reveals almost nothing about himself except to say that as a child, apparently through some accident, he lost the use of his left arm. Otherwise, *The Way of a Pilgrim* tells the story of how the author became a pilgrim, walking the Russian countryside in prayer, reflection, and conversation with those he happened to meet along the way. The central theme of the book is the pilgrim's discovery of—and love for—the Jesus prayer.

The pilgrim explains that one Sunday he went to church and heard a reading from the New Testament's First Epistle of Paul to Timothy, and these words struck him deeply: "Pray without ceasing." The pilgrim pondered how he might fulfill this injunction. So traveling from place to place, whenever he met someone who might have some spiritual knowledge he asked how he might learn to "pray without ceasing." No one could help him until one day he encountered a monk who admonished him: "The Christian is bound to perform many good works, but before all else what he ought to do is pray, for without prayer no other good work whatever can be accomplished."[13]

The monk then said:

> "The continuous interior Prayer of Jesus is a constant uninterrupted calling upon the divine Name of Jesus with the lips, in the spirit, in the heart: while forming a mental picture of His constant presence, and imploring His grace, during every occupation, at all times, in all places, even during sleep. The appeal is couched in these terms, 'Lord Jesus Christ, have mercy on me.' One who accustoms himself to this appeal experiences as a result so deep a consolation and so great a need to offer the prayer always, that he can no longer live without it, and it will continue to voice itself within him of its own accord."[14]

Many months passed and, in spite of his useless left arm, the pilgrim managed to obtain work as a gardener for the summer, with a little hut to live in as part of the agreement. At the end of the summer, the pilgrim began to wander again. He had constantly recited the Jesus prayer while doing his work as a gardener, and on his travels he continued doing this. But it became a source of boredom, and he drew no comfort from it. Still he persisted. Then one day, as if by some special grace, the prayer changed:

> I had the feeling that the Prayer had, so to speak, by its own action passed from my lips to my heart. That is to say, it seemed as though my heart in its ordinary beating began to say the words of the Prayer within at each beat. . . . I gave up saying the Prayer with my lips. I simply listened carefully to what my heart was saying.[15]

It is important to see that there are actually three movements to using this prayer: First, recall that God is present, here and now, all around. Second, put the head in the heart, which simply means to shift the center of attention from the head, where it usually is, to the heart. In fact, these first two parts of the Jesus prayer are the most important. Third, through patient practice the prayer takes on a life of its own, continuing deep in the heart at all times.

Listen to St. Theophan the Recluse, a nineteenth-century Russian mystic:

> In order to keep the mind on one thing by the use of a short prayer, it is necessary to preserve attention and so lead it into the heart: for so long as the mind remains in the head, where thoughts jostle one another, it has no time to concentrate on one thing. But when attention descends into the heart, it attracts all the powers of the soul and body into one point there.[16]

Prayer and spirituality are, first of all, everyday activities. "Spirituality" cannot be separated from "lifestyle."
How we live is how we go about living spiritually, and
our prayerfulness expresses itself in the rhythm of our
heart. Faith has as much to do with our work as it does
with the relatively brief times we spend in formal worship. This is the heart of authentic faith, authentic spirituality, and an authentic approach to prayer.

The Buddhist practice of mindfulness is meant to
help cultivate this everyday approach to living one's religion. The *Diamond Sutra*, one of Buddhism's sacred
writings, says: "Thus shall you think of all this fleeting
world; / A star at dawn, a bubble in a stream; / A flash
of lightning in a summer cloud, / A flickering lamp, a
phantom and a dream" (verse 32).[17] The idea is to remember that all things, even the simplest and most
beautiful, pass away quickly. Only sensitivity to others
and compassion for them are lasting. Therefore, Buddhism teaches the need to practice mindfulness, which
means giving your attention to the effects on others of
your thoughts and actions. Mindfulness includes the
practice of the Five Precepts: "I undertake the rule of
training of refraining from: harming living beings; taking what is not given; misuse of the senses; false speech;
self-intoxication due to alcoholic drink or drugs."[18]

The practice of mindfulness is not, of course, done
for its own sake. Rather, one practices mindfulness in
order to cultivate a spirit of compassion and peace and
to enter more easily into meditation. Utilized in other religious traditions, mindfulness might be understood as
preparing oneself for prayer, for entering into prayerful
loving intimacy with God. The less "scattered" a person

is, the more easily he or she can move from action to contemplation.

Basic to the everyday nature of spirituality in Islam is the need to be forgiving at all times. Muslims refer to God by various names, among them "Compassionate," "Merciful," and "Forgiver." The words *relenting* and *pardoning* are used frequently in Muslim prayers and are often discussed by Muslim spiritual writers. A sacred saying of Islam is: "Is there anyone who seeks my forgiveness, that I might forgive?" According to tradition, Muhammad said, "My heart is clouded until I have sought God's forgiveness seventy times day and night."[19]

Islam sees forgiveness as the heart of a Muslim's everyday spirituality because it goes to the heart of human relationships. If a person is always ready to forgive, then people will get along and life will be peaceful. Muhammad said: "If anyone continually asks pardon, God will show that person a way out of every difficulty and respite from every anxiety, with sustenance from where he least expected it."[20]

The traditional Roman Catholic notion of recollection belongs in an everyday spirituality as well. The idea is to "collect" yourself around a unifying center, namely, your inner union with God in love. Recollection is practiced as a way to "get yourself together" during prayer, but it is also a matter of going through your day with an inner center of peace that cannot be disturbed by external events. "Blessed is the man who can set aside all sources of distraction and perfectly recollect himself," said Thomas à Kempis in the fifteenth-century *Imitation of Christ*.[21]

TRUE FAITH IS COUNTER-CULTURAL

The idea that we should bring our faith and spirituality into the everyday world also carries with it the possibility of conflict, for there are ways in which the world sometimes rejects good in favor of evil. For any authentic spirituality, there is bound to be a counter-cultural element, ways in which the heart and soul of our spiritual experience and beliefs clash with social injustice, cultural superficiality, violence, and the like. This counter-cultural imperative, if we may call it that, is essentially a sensitivity to the difference between what ought to be and what is, between the ideal and the actual. Yet, it depends on the hope that things can change for the better. The result is a dual reaction, one that compels the believer "away" and one that compels the believer "toward." In the New Testament's Gospel of John (chapter 17), Jesus prays for his followers, saying that they do not belong to the world. Yet, he sends them into the world on his behalf. This "in the world but not of it" dynamic is at the heart of the Christian faith, and various Christian traditions interpret it in various ways. At the very least, it means that believers live in the world according to a set of values and standards that will sometimes bring them into conflict with a culture often out of touch with spiritual realities.

Whenever social injustices grip a society, religious people are among the first to protest wrongs. During the war in Vietnam in the 1960s and early 1970s, Buddhist monks in southeast Asia led protests, and Christian and Jewish religious leaders in the United States were prominent in their opposition to the war. The most visible leader of the civil rights movement in the United States was Martin Luther King, Jr., a Baptist minister. During the revolution in Mexico in the 1920s, Roman Catholic priests were among the most active opponents to oppression and persecution. When communism was imposed in eastern Europe following World War II, religious leaders were considered among the most dangerous "enemies of the state" because they stood for humanitarian values that threatened the power of communist governments.

When people want to make of religion and spirituality little more than a source of personal comfort and security, this outward thrust toward justice and peace emerges as a corrective, reminding believers that the purpose of religion and spirituality is more than private, that its social dimension can make the world a better place. Mother Teresa of Calcutta, for instance, saw people dying in the streets, and her deep, intense Catholic faith compelled her to do something about it.

In Judaism, to give charity to the poor is a biblical precept: "If there be among you a needy person . . . you must surely open your hand to him" (Deuteronomy 15:7–8). "You shall maintain him; whether stranger or sojourner, he shall live beside you" (Leviticus 25:35).[22]

All religious teachings lend themselves to a concern for maintaining the health and balance of the natural environment. Buddhist nuns at Chithurst Monastery in England, for instance, restored an ancient English forest that was threatened with extinction. Roman Catholics and other Christians point to the famous Italian saint and mystic Francis of Assisi (c. 1181–1226), whose legendary love for animals and for nature in general remains an inspiration today. Respect for all living things is a well-known teaching of Hinduism, and many Hindu temples daily become the only places where poor people may obtain food to eat.

Judaism, too, has an ecological dimension that encourages respect for the holiness of creation. Contemporary Judaism highlights the duty we have to protect the natural world, and reverence for the land. Indeed, environmental beliefs and practices have been part of the fabric of Jewish life for centuries.

Regardless of the form it takes, however, a balanced spirituality includes the willingness to make the world a better place, even if we risk compromising our own comfort and convenience, even if we risk our very life. Believers support and nourish this dedication to caring for and protecting life and the values that support life by various forms of prayer. This is one of the reasons prayer is central to all religious traditions: it nourishes a mature spirituality that is prepared to bring the values of religion into the real world in whatever ways are necessary. Therefore, the purpose of prayer is not only devotional but practical, as well.

TAKING GOD TO WORK

The daily character of prayer also shows itself in the ways that faith traditions see the sacred as being present in our daily work. A mistaken interpretation of words from the Hebrew Scriptures previously led to a belief among many Christians that God intended work as a punishment for the sin of Adam and Eve:

> And to the man [the Lord] said, "Because
> you have listened to the voice of your wife,

and have eaten of the tree about which I
commanded you, 'You shall not eat of it,'
cursed is the ground because of you; in toil
you shall eat of it all the days of your life;
thorns and thistles it shall bring forth for you;
and you shall eat the plants of the field. By the
sweat of your face you shall eat bread . . .
(Genesis 3:17–19.)

To interpret work as a punishment, however, is to overlook a verse from earlier in the Genesis story that includes work as one of God's gifts to Adam: "The Lord
God took the man and put him in the garden of Eden to
till it and keep it" (2:15). Clearly, then, in the Jewish and
Christian traditions, work is meant to be a part of life in
which people may live their faith.

This may be easy to understand for people whose
work is a source of satisfaction and fulfillment. But what
about people who are not fortunate enough to find work
that is a rewarding part of their existence? Many experience work as little more than a necessary evil, largely because in modern societies work is often dehumanizing.
Yet, even in such conditions, the sacred has an important
role to play. Even when work is unsatisfying or boring, it
still brings us into contact with other people—people
who need respect and compassion. Even when work is
not a source of fulfillment, it is a source of income to support us and our families. Sometimes there is a need to
pray oneself through a bad work experience until other
work can be found.

Those whose work is satisfying and fulfilling do not
find it difficult to perceive the Divine Mystery in their
work experience. A physician, teacher, bus driver, or
computer software developer who loves his or her work

can easily find the holy in the workplace. At the same time, no work is without its shadow side, its sources of frustration or difficulty. So there is always room for personal discipline and tolerance for what we find irritating. There is also always room to bring our work into our prayer and, by doing this, to improve our compassion for others.

For some people, work means *being* an employer. Judaism sees the sacred aspects of being an employer and offers directions about how to act justly:

> It is a Torah commandment to pay the wages of a hired person at the agreed time. Delay constitutes a violation of a Biblical precept: "You must pay him his wages on the same day, before the sun sets" (Deut. 24:15). The reference is to a night laborer. In the case of a day laborer who collects his salary during the night, it says: "The wages of a laborer shall not remain with you all night until morning" (Lev. 19:13).[23]

At the same time, Judaism looks at the employer/ employee relationship not just from the perspective of justice but from that of mercy, as well. Say an employee causes his or her employer some loss. Even if the loss happens through negligence, or in such a way that the employee is legally responsible for causing some damage, the employer is morally obligated to let the employee off the hook, "so you may go in the way of goodness" (Proverbs 2:20).[24] Not only that, but if the employee is a poor person, the employer is obliged to pay his or her wages for the day of the offense, as well.

Just as Judaism cautions the employer not to cheat

on the wages of the employee, so the employee is to do his or her work conscientiously, of course, and not waste time on the job. This may seem like a discussion of ethics for the world of work, but in truth it is a practical application of spirituality and dedication to prayer to the everyday world. To act in such a manner, as either an employer or an employee, is to let the spirit of prayer surface in the everyday world and to overcome the sacred/secular dichotomy.

All kinds of work call for an increasing sensitivity to the presence of the Divine Mystery in one's work, and therefore there is a need for an ongoing dedication to a life of prayer.

Each form of work has many unique dimensions, of course. A teacher's work is not the same as a physician's work, and a truck driver's work is not the same as a computer technician's work. Each will find unique ways to discover God in the workplace; each will find unique spiritual issues to deal with. Each will discover ways in which prayer fits into his or her workday.

In the mid-1960s, the Second Vatican Council of the Roman Catholic Church pointed out the sacred connections between the workaday world and spirituality:

> That [people], working in harmony, should renew the temporal order and make it increasingly more perfect: such is God's design for the world.
>
> All that goes to make up the temporal order: personal and family values, culture, economic interests, the trades and professions, institutions of the political community, international relations, and so on, as well as their gradual development—all these are not merely helps

> to [humanity's] last end; they possess a value
> of their own, placed in them by God, whether
> considered individually or as parts of the inte-
> gral temporal structure: "And God saw all that
> he had made and found it very good" (Genesis
> 1:31).[25]

All religions understand that if we are to be authentically spiritual it must happen in the context of everyday
life. Islam, for instance, explicitly places everyday life at
its exact center:

> The distinctive thing about Islam is not its
> ideal but the detailed prescriptions it sets forth
> for achieving it. . . . Westerners who define re-
> ligion in terms of personal experience would
> never be understood by Muslims, whose reli-
> gion calls them to establish a specific kind of
> social order. Islam joins faith to politics, reli-
> gion to society, inseparably.[26]

Islam is highly sensitive to the physical and material
basis of human existence. A person who is hungry,
thirsty, or without adequate shelter or clothing finds it
difficult to pray or think about "higher" spiritual concerns. Muslims tell of a man who came to Muhammad in
tears and told him that his mother had died. What best
alms, he wondered, could he give away for the good of
his mother's soul? Muhammad, quite aware of the heat
of the desert, replied immediately, "Water! Dig a well . . .
[in her memory], and give water to the thirsty."[27]

Islam teaches that for a society to be healthy, material goods must be distributed fairly. Islam has no objec-
tion to the profit motive, competition among businesses,

or entrepreneurial creativity. In fact, it encourages them so much that sometimes the Qur'an is called "a businessman's book."[28] Islam has no problem with someone working harder than a neighbor or being more successful than others. It does insist, however, that all this be balanced by fair play and by a compassion that gives generously to the less fortunate. Islam requires that annually a portion of one's wealth be given to the poor.

Prayer cannot be authentic unless it brings transcendent values and a divine perspective into everyday ethics and ordinary life. The Buddha himself told about a tailor who cheated his customers and congratulated himself on being more clever than others. One day the tailor suffered a great loss because of his unfair practices.

The Buddha told this story to show that dishonesty leads to disaster. He explained that in a previous life, the tailor was a crane who lived near a pond. When the dry season came, the crane asked the fish that lived in the pond if they feared that the pond would dry up. The fish replied that they were, indeed, afraid. "I know a fine, large lake, which never becomes dry," said the crane. "Would you not like me to carry you there in my beak?"

The fish did not trust the crane, since cranes love to eat fish. But finally, a large carp took a chance for his fellow fish so he could test the crane's honesty. The crane took the carp in his beak, flew to the lake so the carp could see it, then flew back to the pond with the carp in safety. The fish were delighted and agreed to let the crane carry them all to the lake.

The crane took the fish in his beak one by one, flew off, and stopped each time to devour the fish he was carrying. When he had eaten all the fish, he returned to the pond. The last resident was a lobster. The crane now offered to carry the lobster to the lake. "How will you do that?" asked the lobster. "I am too big to fit securely in your beak, and you will surely drop me." The crane argued that he would hold the lobster tightly, but the lobster refused.

The lobster was certain that no crane with a fish in his beak is about to let that fish go free. Surely the crane had eaten all the fish and had a similar fate in mind for the lobster. Still, the lobster liked the idea of leaving the pond to live in the lake. So the lobster talked the crane into letting him hold on to the crane's neck with one of his powerful claws so he would not fall during the flight. The crane agreed, and off he flew with the lobster holding on to his neck. When the lobster saw that the crane was not flying toward the lake, he asked him why. The crane replied that he was no taxi service, and he was going to eat the lobster just as he had eaten all the fish.

The lobster said to the crane that the fish had all died from their own stupidity. But he was not so stupid. "If I die, you will die, too, for I will cut off your head in midair with my claw." With that the lobster tightened his grip on the crane's neck, and the crane began to cry. He begged the lobster not to cut off his head.

The lobster said that if the crane would fly him down to the lake he would let the crane go free. The crane alighted at the lake's edge, and immediately the lobster cut the crane's neck and slipped into the water.

When the Buddha finished his story, he added, "Not now only was this man outwitted in this way, but in other existences, too, by his own intrigues."[29]

Prayer may be distinguished from contemplative prayer or meditation—which we will discuss in Chapter 3—by describing prayer as the silent or spoken, solitary or communal, recitation of prayerful words or formulas. The blessings Judaism offers for so many aspects of everyday life belong in this category. This morning prayer is one example: "I thank Thee, O King, who lives for always and who, as I awaken, has in mercy returned my soul to me; we can ever trust in Thee."[30]

THE MANY VARIETIES OF PRAYER

Prayers may be traditional and formulaic, or they may be original and spontaneous. The Lord's Prayer, which begins, "Our Father, who art in heaven," is the most commonly used Christian prayer, but there are many others, as well. Roman Catholic devotion to Mary, the mother of Jesus, expresses itself in the most commonly used Marian prayer, which begins, "Hail Mary, full of grace, the Lord is with thee." Similar prayers and blessings exist in the Islamic, Hindu, and Buddhist traditions. One Hindu prayer, for example, the sacred *Gayatri* mantra, is to be recited by all Hindus at sunrise, noon, and sunset: "Om. Oh terrestrial sphere. Oh sphere of space. Oh celestial sphere. Let us contemplate the splendor of the solar spirit, the divine creator. May He guide our minds."[31]

The prayers associated with religious rites and rituals are all part of the discipline of prayer. This discipline enables the believer to express and nourish devotion to the Divine Mystery and maintain a dedication to ongoing personal transformation.

Muslims begin every action with a formulaic prayer, "In the Name of God Most Merciful, Most Compassionate," end every action with another formulaic prayer, "Praise be to God," and express resignation to what has happened, regardless of what it is, with yet another prayer, "What God has willed." In planning future actions, Muslims pray, "if God wills."

"To pray is to change," writes a Christian author. "Prayer is the central avenue God uses to transform us. If we are unwilling to change, we will abandon prayer as a noticeable characteristic of our lives. The closer we come to the heartbeat of God, the more we see our need and the more we desire to be conformed to Christ."[32]

Prayer exists as a discipline to help the believer maintain his or her relationship with the divine. Those pray who admit that they have a *need* to pray.

> "I will pray only when I am moved to pray" is the argument heard from those who object to regular prayer. Suffice it to recall the proverbial story of the soldier in the foxhole who, when he wanted to pray, did not know what to say or how to say it. To pray with true sincerity, to reach spiritual heights as a result of true prayer, is not easy. It requires training and practice. It is an art in itself.
>
> While it is true that not every time an observant Jew fulfills his prayer obligations does he reach these noble heights, the likelihood of such experiences, and the occasions on which he *will* experience such heights, are always greater for him than for the one who *waits* to be inspired.[33]

The practice of prayer is a learned skill, every bit as much as riding a bicycle is a learned skill. But, like riding a bicycle, once learned it is not something one is likely to forget. We become prayerful by cultivating the *habit* of prayer, and a habit is cultivated by repeating certain behaviors. Among the most universal approaches to prayer is the simple custom of saying appropriate prayers in the morning and again at night. The simplest, easiest, most basic way to be prayerful is simply to cultivate the habit of morning and night prayer, using prayers available from the religious tradition in which you are rooted, or into which you were born. In time, you may wish to develop your prayer discipline further, perhaps adding a midday prayer.

The primary purpose of prayer is to cultivate one's relationship with the Divine Mystery. We pray for much the same reason that we spend time and talk with people we love or care for, except that in prayer the other party in the relationship is much more than another human being. Still, we pray to "be with" God, Allah, the Divine Mystery, the Holy One upon whom our existence depends. And because prayer is a discipline, we are free to learn about prayer even as we pray from day to day. We often overlook that we learn *by praying,* but we also learn about our relationship with the Divine Mystery along the way so our prayer grows and deepens. A Christian author reports, for example:

> One of the most liberating experiences in my life came when I understood that prayer involved a learning process. I was set free to question, to experiment, even to fail, for I knew I was learning.[34]

In Islam, one of the primary purposes of daily prayer is to keep one's life in perspective. The Qur'an presents this as one of the toughest lessons anyone must learn. People just cannot seem to live in a manner appropriate for creatures who brought neither themselves nor their world into existence. Instead, they keep trying to live as if they were the center of the universe, and this causes nothing but trouble for them and for others. "When we ask, then, why Muslims pray, a partial answer is: in response to life's natural impulse to give thanks for its existence. The deeper answer, however, is . . . to keep life in perspective—to see it objectively, which involves acknowledging human creatureliness before its Creator."[35] In other words, Muslims pray in order to submit their will to God's will in all things.

In Zen Buddhism, our ultimate spiritual purpose is satori (enlightenment), the realization of the connectedness of all things. Prayer and meditation are undertaken for the sake of mindfulness, which means learning to live from our deepest center regardless of what we happen to be doing at the moment. Sometimes mindfulness can lead to satori. As always, there are many Zen stories that illustrate how enlightenment can suddenly come to one who learns mindfulness through prayer and meditation:

> When Banzan was walking through the market he overheard a conversation between a butcher and his customer.
>
> "Give me the best piece of meat you have," said the customer.
>
> "Everything in my shop is the best," replied the butcher. "You cannot find here any piece of meat that is not the best."
>
> At these words Banzan became enlightened.[36]

All this may lead one to conclude that prayer is terribly complicated, too difficult for the average person to learn.

On the contrary, we should never make prayer too complicated. Christianity responds to this mistake by pointing out that Jesus taught his disciples to turn to God as little children turn to a loving father. Prayer should be, above all, an expression of trust: trust in God, trust in Allah, trust in Life, trust in the Divine Mystery which, or who, is the source and goal of our being and the being of all things.

Ordinary, everyday prayer is easy. Thomas Merton once remarked, with disarming simplicity, "How I pray is breathe."[37] In the mid-1960s, when the great Jewish philosopher Abraham Joshua Heschel marched with Martin Luther King, Jr., in Selma, Alabama, he said, "My feet were praying."[38] That's how simple prayer is. Ultimately, all prayer is about ordinary, everyday life, as this prayer-poem by contemporary Zen Buddhist monk Thich Nhat Hanh illustrates:

> Waking up this morning, I smile
> Twenty-four brand new hours are before me.
> I vow to live fully in each moment
> And to look at all beings with eyes of
>   compassion.[39]

The various faith traditions all agree that if we do not carry the spirit of prayer into the everyday world, prayer becomes little more than a game we play for our own private purposes. We find the sacred in the ordinary, and we find our way in the world by making prayer an integral part of everyday life. The first well from which we draw spiritual nourishment for everyday life is the faith tradition to which we belong. But we can deepen our prayer by consulting the wisdom of other faith traditions, as well.

Chapter 2

The Spirit of Prayerfulness and Playfulness

Picture yourself in the middle of a gathering for purely social purposes. Maybe you are attending a convention and you're in a large ballroom. Hundreds of people are milling about, drinks in hand. The chatter level is high, and a three- or four-piece band, over in a corner of the room, is laying down some lively tunes. You are part of a group of, say, four people, none of whom are close friends. The topic of conversation is sales figures, hiring practices, or the new division manager. Out of the blue, one of the people in your little group declares that he or she has been "praying about it."

It's as if this person had just sprouted a second head or a third arm. "Mm," they say. "Mm-hm. (Pause.) Oh, I see someone over there I need to check with about something. Nice talking with you. I'll catch you later."

No one wants to offend the person who has just mentioned prayer, but the topic is a serious one and, well, this is a light social gathering, and we don't want to discuss, you know, religion. Sure, everyone is thinking, I'm a religious person, too, but there is religion and there is religion, and mine is in another part of the playing field. Besides, prayer is a serious topic, not something you bring up in the middle of a group of people, all of whom are sipping various alcoholic beverages. The two don't mix.

This response to a mention of prayer is typical. Both spiritually-minded and spiritually indifferent people tend to think of prayer as a "heavy" topic. But, we have been misled. We could do ourselves a service by watching a scene in an old Monty Python movie, *The Meaning of Life*—a scene that rightly deflates overly solemn ideas abut religion. An actor dressed in the formal liturgical garb of a bishop stands in the nave of a huge Gothic cathedral and prays aloud: "Oh God, you are so big! You are really, really big! You are just *so big!*"

One point of this Monty Python jest, of course, is to make fun of a too-solemn understanding of prayer. It is appropriate for prayer to be dignified, but prayer is much bigger than this, much more adaptable, more flexible—more *human*. The *spirit* of authentic prayerfulness is as wide as life and the universe, as deep as the human heart, and it belongs not just in a cathedral but everywhere. The spirit of prayerfulness is, in fact, much bigger than the explicit act of praying. Sure, we pray sometimes. But the spirit of prayerfulness can be present and accounted for in all kinds of situations where no one is praying at all.

There is, of course, an important distinction here. There is prayer, and there is the *spirit* of prayerfulness.

The spirit of prayerfulness is much more basic than the explicit act of prayer. The *spirit* of prayerfulness is foundational to the very act of praying. In other words, before a person can pray authentically, before prayer can be more than a matter of pious words and pious gestures, that person needs to have a prior or underlying experience of the Divine Mystery in the world—a conviction, based on personal experience, that God is real. This is where the spirit of prayerfulness originates—with the experience of God's presence.

Many people who are religious in a merely cultural or formal sense, and many people who claim no religious or spiritual sensibilities at all, have never experienced the Divine Mystery for themselves. They have never had an experience of the divine presence.

This does not mean that before we can pray we must have some sort of "mystical experience." One of the most famous examples of this kind of experience is that of Blaise Pascal, a seventeenth-century Catholic philosopher and mathematician. After Pascal's death, discovered sewn into the lining of his coat was a piece of paper on which he had described his own mystical experience: "FIRE. 'God of Abraham, God of Isaac, God of Jacob,' not of philosophers and scholars. Certainty, certainty, heartfelt joy, peace. God of Jesus Christ. . . . The world forgotten, and everything except God. . . . Greatness of the human soul. . . . Joy, joy, joy, tears of joy."[1]

Most people do not have the kind of experience Pascal described. But all the same, we can experience God's loving presence and respond to it prayerfully. What many people do not realize is that all they need to do is ask, and when we ask we discover that all along we have had what we are asking for.

The enlightenment experience of the Buddha under the bodhi tree; Muhammad's experience of having the Qur'an "fall" on him because its words had such weight; Moses' encounter with God in the burning bush; Jesus' forty days of being tempted in the desert, at the end of which angels ministered to him; and the remarkable experiences of many great mystics and holy men and women through the centuries—we tend to think of these as extraordinary. In one sense, they *are* extraordinary because few people are mystics in the sense that these people were. All the same, everyone has the capacity to experience the Divine Mystery if they are willing to make room for this experience to happen, and if they are willing to recognize the sacred in the ordinary.

In Judaism's Hasidic tradition, daily prayer and mysticism are paramount. Hasidism teaches that God is to be found in every dimension of life, not just through the Commandments, and it places an emphasis on emotion and joyful devotion to God. At the heart of the Hasidic tradition is the doctrine of *devekut*, which means "attachment," in the sense of being always with God. This is an ideal not just for the few but for everyone.

A well-known example of the doctrine of *devekut* ("devotion" or "clinging to God") in action is the scene from the musical *Fiddler on the Roof* where Tevye, the nineteenth-century Jewish milkman, pours out his soul to God in prayer. His words reflect an everyday closeness with God, a feeling that Tevye and God are like two peas in a pod, not distant, but daily companions. Tevye feels perfectly natural about complaining to God, questioning Him:

Dear God, you made many, many poor people.
I realize, of course, that it's no shame to be

poor. But it's no great honor, either! So what would have been so terrible if I had a small fortune?

Tevye then sings his song "If I Were a Rich Man," and the concluding words of the song summarize his entire prayer: "Would it spoil some vast, eternal plan, if I were a wealthy man?"[2]

Tevye and his song reflect beautifully the Hasidic doctrine of *devekut*. Tevye's God is not a God who is far removed but an everyday companion and the source of both poverty and wealth, fortune and misfortune.

GETTING CLOSER TO GOD

Islam, too, embraces the concept that the experience of God is not to be reserved for ascetics dwelling on mountaintops. The Qur'an speaks of those "whom neither commerce nor trafficking diverts from the remembrance of God." (24:37). In Islam, religion is in the heart, which is also the dwelling place of love of God. What matters is "the knowledge that we utterly depend on God."[3]

Hinduism focuses on our experience of God in many manifestations. Still, behind all the gods and goddesses there is the One who is present in all creatures. "The disciple who participates in me," says the Bhagavad Gita, "who am present in all creatures, and who, established in Unity, is yet engaged in all kinds of occupations, abides in me."[4]

Buddhism is known for its monasteries filled with monks, but Buddhism leads adherents to seek enlightenment by living everyday life according to the Four

Noble Truths and the Noble Eightfold Path, and to reject all forms of injury: "Not to do evil, to cultivate good, to purify one's mind, this is the teaching of the Buddhas."[5]

Native African religions, too, relate to a God who is very close to, and part of, everyday experience. A prayer from Rwanda and Burundi echoes the pain of a childless woman, and she is not reluctant to express her feelings, thoughts, and anger, even to God:

> I don't know for what Imana [God] is punishing me. If I could meet with him, I would kill him. Imana, why are you punishing me? . . . Couldn't you even give me one little child, Yo-oh-o! I am dying in anguish! If only I could meet you and pay you out! Come on, let me kill you! . . . O Imana, you have deserted me! Yo-o-o![6]

The woman who speaks this prayer is obviously angry, and she is not intimidated, even by God. She is so disappointed and angry about being childless that if she met God face to face she would try to "kill him." This is a spirit of prayerfulness that insists on being honest with God and even on raging in God's face when conditions seem to warrant it.

The lesson to learn from this kind of prayer is the importance of making prayer more than a pious activity. Sometimes prayer needs to have an "in your face" attitude toward what the Monty Python character calls a "really *big*" God.

In a unique fashion, American Indian spirituality "is characterized by a worldview according to which the natural, social, and spiritual dimensions are understood to be profoundly integrated."[7] This makes the American Indian spirit of prayerfulness especially admirable when it comes to integrating it into everyday life. It is risky to generalize about "all" American Indian cultures. Still, many American Indian cultures do share the perspective of the Oglala visionary Black Elk: "We regard all created beings as sacred and important, for everything has a *wochangi* or influence which can be given to us."[8]

Traditional American Indian spirituality tends to see healing, hunting, and farming as spiritual activities. Indeed, traditional American Indian religion is monotheistic and embodies a holistic spirituality that contrasts with a highly rationalized Western religious consciousness. Consequently, the traditional American Indian spirit of prayer blends with a deep awareness of the sacredness of the natural world.

Sherman Alexie is both a Spokane/Coeur d'Alene Indian and a Catholic poet, novelist, and filmmaker. Alexie reflects a deep awareness of the holiness of nature in his poem "Drum as Love, Fear, and Prayer":

> Then she tells me Jesus is
> still here
> because Jesus was
> once here
>
> and parts of Jesus are
> still floating in the air.
> She tells me Jesus' DNA is
> part of the collective DNA.
>
> She tells me we are all part
> of Jesus, we are all Jesus

> in part. She tells me to breathe deep
> during all of our storms
> because you can sometimes taste Jesus
> in a good, hard rain.[9]

In his novel *Reservation Blues*, Sherman Alexie offers another example of the Native American spirit of prayerfulness which taps deeply into a holistic vision of life and the world—in this case, contemporary life on a reservation. Alexie's character, Thomas Builds-the-Fire, walks outside one night, under the stars:

> "Hello," he said to the night sky. He wanted to say the first word of a prayer or a joke. A prayer and a joke often sound alike on the reservation.
> "Help," he said to the ground. He knew the words to a million songs: Indian, European, African, Mexican, Asian. He sang "Stairway to Heaven" in four different languages but never knew where that staircase stood. He sang the same Indian songs continually but never sang them correctly. He wanted to make his guitar sound like a waterfall, like a spear striking salmon, but his guitar only sounded like a guitar. He wanted the songs, the stories, to save everybody.
>
> "Father," he said to the crickets, who carried their own songs to worry about.[10]

The spirit of prayerfulness has roots in our sense that the Divine Mystery is present at the roots of our own being and at the heart of everything that is, was, or ever will be. God can no more be separated from the most obscure wildflower growing on a wilderness hillside than from the most distant star twinkling in the night sky. The divine presence can no more be separated from my own self than from the person sitting next to me on a bus or subway train. God is all in all, and everything is in God. The experience of this reality is the source of the spirit of prayerfulness in everyday life.

Cultivating this spirit is not as difficult as it may seem. The Jesus prayer (discussed in the previous chapter) is one way to do this. Another is the practice of the presence of God. Brother Lawrence, who was cook in a seventeenth-century monastery in France, wrote eloquently yet simply of how he learned to cultivate living in the presence of God as he went about his ordinary daily tasks. "If I were a preacher," Brother Lawrence wrote, "I should preach nothing else but the practice of the presence of God. If I were a [spiritual] director, I should recommend it to everyone, so much do I believe it is essential and even easy."[11]

So convinced was Brother Lawrence of God's closeness in everyday experience that he declared that God "is nearer to us than we think."[12] The practice of the presence of God, to Brother Lawrence, was not difficult or esoteric but the most ordinary of disciplines:

> It is not needful always to be in church to be with God. We can make a chapel of our heart, to which we can from time to time withdraw to have gentle, humble, loving communion with him. Everyone is able to have these familiar conversations with God, some more, some less—he knows our capabilities. Let us

make a start. Perhaps he only waits for us to
make one whole-hearted resolve. Courage![13]

Brother Lawrence's book about God's presence consists
of conversations with the monk written down later by
someone else, letters written by Brother Lawrence to others, and "The Spiritual Principles of Brother Lawrence,"
written by the monk himself. In one of the conversations,
Brother Lawrence summarizes his understanding of the
spirit of prayerfulness in one sentence: "The time of
prayer was, he said, no different for him than any
other."[14] And again, in the "Spiritual Principles": "The
time of action does not differ from that of prayer. I possess God as peacefully in the bustle of my kitchen, where
sometimes several people are asking me for difficult
things at the same time, as I do upon my knees before the
Holy Sacrament."

This sense of the sameness of the unity of all time,
and of God's presence in all times and places, led
Brother Lawrence to experience all times as prayerful.
"He gave thought neither to death, nor his sins, nor Par-
adise nor Hell, but only to do small things for the love of
God. Great things, he said, he was not able to do."[15]

Brother Lawrence was careful to point out that God
is present not just in times of comfort and joy. Quite the
contrary, "God is often nearer to us in our times of sickness and infirmity, than when we are enjoying perfect
health."[16] For Brother Lawrence, all times are prayerful
times because God is in all times where we happen to be
at the moment. The challenge is one of awareness on our
part, to learn to be in the divine presence no matter what
we are doing or where we are. In one of the most charming sections of his entire book, Brother Lawrence says:

I turn my little omelette in the pan for the love
of God. When it is finished, if I have nothing to
do, I prostrate myself on the ground and worship my God, who gave me the grace to make
it, after which I arise happier than a king.
When I can do nothing else, it is enough to
have picked up a straw for the love of God.[17]

True Prayerfulness Transcends Religious Institutions

The spirit of prayerfulness in everyday life is what religion is about. The ultimate purpose of "institutional" or
"organized" religion is to nourish and guide people on
the deepest spiritual and human level. But that, unfortu-
nately, is not how people often perceive religion. A series
of "Peanuts" cartoon strips by Charles Schulz illustrates
this problem.[18] In the series, Peppermint Patty lies on the
ground, her head resting on a rock, while her friend Marcie lies nearby. Suddenly, a butterfly flits along and lands
on Peppermint Patty's nose. After a few amusing ex-
changes between Patty and Marcie, the butterfly remains
on Patty's nose, and she falls asleep. Marcie blows on the
butterfly, and it flies away. Peppermint Patty wakes up
and asks what happened to the butterfly.

"A miracle, sir!" Marcie exclaims. (She has the odd
habit of calling Peppermint Patty "sir.") "While you
were asleep it turned into an angel, and flew away!!"

Immediately Peppermint Patty tells Charlie Brown,

Lucy, Linus, and her other friends about her "miracle." Patty concludes that she has been chosen to bring a special message to the world. "Why else would a butterfly land on my nose," she wonders, "and then turn into an angel?" Still, Patty is not sure what message she is meant to bring to the world. "How about this?" she suggests to Linus. "If there's a foul ball behind third base, it's the shortstop's play!"

So much for profound spiritual messages for the world. Still, Peppermint Patty is determined to tell about her "miracle." She goes to a church office, where a woman gives her an information sheet about Sunday School. In the next strip, Peppermint Patty lies on the ground, exhausted. "You look tired, sir," says Marcie.

"I've been to three tabernacles, fourteen churches, and two temples."

"No one wanted to hear about your miracle?"

"All I got was a bunch of tracts and this," Patty replies, holding up a sheet of paper. "'Want to receive a blessing?'" she reads. "'Donate to our new lawn sprinkling system.'"

Anyone who wonders why so many people are genuinely concerned about their spirituality and about prayer, but keep their distance from "organized" religion, can take a lesson from this series of "Peanuts" comic strips. Peppermint Patty has had what she believes is a genuine spiritual experience. Yes, she has been fooled by Marcie, since there was no angel, just a butterfly. The point is that Patty was serious about her experience and wanted someone to take her seriously, yet when she approached religious institutions she received no hearing at all, just information about institutional programs. Even worse was a flyer she was handed that tied getting a blessing to giving money to buy a sprinkler system. Many people perceive "organized religion" as being uninterested in precisely what religion is supposed to be all about: nourishing spirituality and supporting the cultivation of the spirit of prayerfulness. Yes, religion is institutionalized, and that is unavoidable. To expect otherwise is naive. But "organized religion" needs to keep its priorities straight. Fund-raising campaigns and committees are of secondary importance. If institutional religion loses sight of its primary mission— cultivating spirituality and the spirit of prayerfulness— if it becomes little more than a social movement, a support community, or a charitable organization, then it loses its soul and has no further right to exist.

The primary mission of "organized religion" is to help people see that religion is not supposed to be an end in itself. Religion should always point beyond itself to the Other, to the Divine Mystery, to God. A congregation needs a building, a church, a temple, a synagogue, a mosque, in which to hold communal worship. But the purpose of the building is to nourish spirituality and the spirit of prayerfulness. When newcomers arrive, à la Peppermint Patty, and want to talk about spiritual issues they regard as important, the first response should not be an invitation to give money or get involved in a "program" of some sort. The first response should be a welcoming hand and a willingness to listen *offered in a context of worship and spiritual devotion*. It should be immediately evident to all newcomers or visitors that the Divine Mystery is what this institution and this religion are about. Everything else comes second, third, and fourth.

Many key people in institutional religion insist that

even religions must "live in the real world." They have bills to pay, repairs to make, programs to support, payrolls to meet. Of course, they are sincere on all counts. But often they are like Linus in another "Peanuts" strip. "When I get big, I'd like to be a prophet," Linus says to Charlie Brown.

"That's a fine ambition," Charlie Brown replies. "The world can always use a few good prophets. The only trouble is that most of them turn out to be *false* prophets."

"Maybe," Linus says, "I could be a *sincere* false prophet."[19]

Organized religion must constantly be on guard against becoming a sincere false prophet. Sincerity counts for something only when proper priorities are maintained, with the highest ideals at the top of the list. Classical Protestant Christianity contributes to this discussion what is sometimes called the Protestant Principle. Basically, this principle warns against making an absolute out of worshiping anything but God. This means that we may substitute nothing for the Divine Mystery. Not sacred writings, not religious rituals or symbols, not official religious teachings, not religious institutions, not personal religious experience. Thus, no particular way of praying may ever become the only acceptable way to pray. Human beings are so unique that it is crucial for each of us to find our unique spiritual way, even within a particular religious tradition.

Not all Hindus follow exactly the same path, not all Christians go about being Christian in identical ways, Buddhism takes a variety of forms, and the same goes for anyone regardless of religion. In other words, the Protestant Principle is a source of liberty and flexibility.

To accept this principle is to free yourself to cultivate a spirit of prayerfulness in whatever ways best nourish your own experience of the Divine Mystery.

DIVINE PLAYFULNESS

Ultimately, the Protestant Principle liberates people to have a spirituality that is not only prayerful but playful. As the Catholic monk and author Thomas Merton once wrote:

> What is serious to men is often very trivial in the sight of God. What in God might appear to us as "play" is perhaps what He Himself takes most seriously. At any rate the Lord plays and diverts Himself in the garden of His creation, and if we could let go of our own obsession with what we think is the meaning of it all, we might be able to hear His call and follow Him in His mysterious, cosmic dance. We do not have to go very far to catch echoes of that game, and of that dancing. When we are alone on a starlit night; when by chance we see the migrating birds in autumn descending on a grove of junipers to rest and eat; when we see children in a moment when they are really children; when we know love in our own hearts; or when like the Japanese poet Bashō we hear an old frog land in a quiet pond with a solitary splash—at such times the awakening, the turning inside out of all values, the "newness," the emptiness and the purity of

vision that make themselves evident, provide
a glimpse of the cosmic dance.[20]

G. K. Chesterton was an Anglican who later became a
Roman Catholic. Chesterton captured well the Christian
perception of a playful God: "There was some one thing
that was too great for God to show us when He walked
upon our earth; and I have sometimes fancied that it was
His mirth."[21]

Virtually all the great religious traditions make
room for a playful prayerfulness that reflects the Divine
Mystery as Something More than Cosmic Seriousness.
Playfulness is the natural consequence when we live according to a religion that cultivates joy. This joyful playfulness is not mere "fun," however, as the dominant
secular culture understands it. It is not a superficial
"joy" that comes from remaining free from personal
commitments, especially permanent commitments.
Rather, it is a playfulness that results precisely from permanent dedication to a cause higher than the self. The
Buddhist story of the Marriage Feast in Jambūnanda is
a good example.[22]

According to the story, a man on the eve of his
wedding thought how wonderful it would be if the
Buddha could be present at the wedding. To his wonder,
the Buddha did walk by the man's house. When the two
met, the Buddha read what was in the man's heart and
agreed to attend the wedding. The bridegroom invited
the Buddha and the many monks in his retinue to enter
his house and eat. "While the holy men ate, the meats
and drinks remained undiminished, and the host
thought to himself: 'How wondrous is this! I should
have had plenty for all my friends and relatives. Would
that I had invited them all.'"[23]

Even as this thought entered the bridegroom's mind, all his relatives and friends entered his house, and even though the house was small there was still room for everyone. There was also more than enough food and drink for all, and "the Blessed One" [the Buddha] was pleased to see so many guests full of good cheer and he quickened them and gladdened them with words of truth, proclaiming the bliss of righteousness."[24]

The Buddha said:

> The greatest happiness which a mortal man can imagine is the bond of marriage that ties together two loving hearts. But there is a greater happiness still: it is the embrace of truth. Death will separate husband and wife, but death will never affect him who has es-poused the truth.
>
> Therefore be married unto the truth and live with the truth in holy wedlock. The husband who loves his wife and desires for a union that shall be everlasting must be faithful to her so as to be like truth itself, and she will rely upon him and revere him and minister unto him. And the wife who loves her husband and de-sires a union that shall be everlasting must be faithful to him so as to be like truth itself; and he will place his trust in her, he will provide for her. Verily, I say unto you, their children will become like unto their parents and will bear witness to their happiness.[25]

The story concludes by remarking that everyone present "was strengthened in his spiritual life, and recognized the sweetness of a life of righteousness; and they took refuge in the Buddha, the Dharma [religion], and the Sangha [Buddhist community]."[26]

Lasting spiritual joy comes from making commitments and from being faithful to those commitments. A joy that results in prayerful playfulness comes not from keeping all your options open but from accepting the truth that it is not possible to have it all. Only by making and keeping promises does the human heart find light, joy, and peace.

COMMITMENT LEADS TO FREEDOM

It seems to be a paradox to say that liberation comes from binding ourselves, that freedom comes from commitment. Yet, human experience shows that people who refuse to choose find themselves imprisoned in the worst way possible. They are imprisoned in the prison of the self. This is why marriage is better than promiscuity, and why it is necessary to be committed to one religious tradition if you are to attain any significant spiritual depth. The person in a committed relationship sacrifices variety for intimacy. The religious person discovers that only by choosing one religious tradition is deep union with God possible. Once the commitment is made—to one person or to one religious tradition—the door swings open to deep joy and prayerful playfulness.

Religious traditions deeply distrust a culture that promises fulfillment and joy as a result of accumulating possessions, wealth, and material comfort. This naturally leads to a distrust of the promise that technology holds the answers to all human misery. One of the

clearest responses to technology comes from the tradition of Sabbath observance in Judaism.

> To persons looking in from the outside . . . the
> Sabbath might appear to be restrictive. A cur-
> sory acquaintance with its restrictions might
> lead one to assume that it is an austere day for
> those who observe it, a day lacking joy and
> spirit. Yet experienced from within, it is just
> the reverse. It serves as a glorious release from
> weekday concerns, routine pressures, and
> even secular recreation. It is a day of peaceful
> tranquility, inner joy and spiritual uplift, ac-
> companied by song and cheer.[27]

Life is not meant to be grim business, and cultivating a
spirit of prayerful playfulness helps the human heart experience this firsthand. The spirit of playfulness sees divine play throughout the universe. It stands by a
mountain stream and watches God playing in the gur-
gling eddies of the stream as it passes over rocks, around
the roots of trees, and under the overhanging riverbank.
The spirit of divine play whistles silently among the
stars, and in their own bumbling way, humans in space
shuttles drift playfully in space, marveling at the earth
far below.

The Divine Mystery plays in the most ordinary
places: in squirrels chasing each other around a city
park, in the chirps of sparrows perched in trees, even in
the clank and growl of a garbage truck as it crawls down
the street. In all of these, the prayerful, watchful ob-
server can find inspiration for reflective prayer.

In all these, and more, Hinduism sees *lila*, "the play
of the Divine in its Cosmic Dance—untiring, unending,

resistless, yet ultimately beneficent, with a grace born of infinite vitality."[28] Indeed, in Hinduism, the fact that there are many religions is yet another sign of God at play. Of the variety of gods and goddesses who reveal the many aspects of the One God, Ramakrishna said:

> There was a man who worshiped Shiva but hated all other deities. One day Shiva appeared to him and said, "I shall never be pleased with you so long as you hate the other gods." But the man was inexorable. After a few days Shiva again appeared to him and said, "I shall never be pleased with you so long as you hate." The man kept silent. After a few days Shiva again appeared to him. This time one side of his body was that of Shiva, and the other side that of Vishnu. The man was half pleased and half displeased. He laid his offerings on the side representing Shiva, and did not offer anything to the side representing Vishnu. Then Shiva said, "Your bigotry is unconquerable. I, by assuming this dual aspect, tried to convince you that all gods and goddesses are but various aspects of the one Absolute Brahman."[29]

To cultivate prayerful playfulness is also to cultivate playful prayerfulness. This is an approach to daily prayer that worships the Lord of the universe with a light heart, with a sense that whatever the future may hold—especially if the future looks dark and forbidding—union with the divine, if it is real, can only lead to a joyful spirit. This is the direct opposite of a religion—of whatever kind—that insists on a grim outlook on life and the world. For if our religion becomes a dark storm cloud that hangs over our heads, then that religion has little to do with the God who plays and dances in the shining leaves of the trees on a summer morning and on the tops of the highest, treacherous, snow-capped mountains of the Himalayas.

A playful, prayerful spirit is basic to a religious outlook on life, for this spirit says that we do not worship our religion. Rather, we worship God alone: the Divine Mystery. Therefore, the authentically religious spirit transcends dichotomies. G. K. Chesterton, a great English Catholic writer of the early twentieth century, was a champion of prayerful playfulness. He wrote:

> When somebody says that a fast is the opposite to a feast, and yet both seem to be sacred to us, some of us will always be moved merely to say, "Yes," and relapse into an unobjectionable grin. When the anxious ethical inquirer says, "Christmas is devoted to merry-making, to eating meat and drinking wine, and yet you encourage this pagan and materialistic enjoyment," you or I will be tempted to say, "Quite right, my boy," and leave it at that. When he then says, looking even more worried, "Yet you admire men for fasting in caves and deserts and denying themselves ordinary pleasures; you are clearly committed . . . to the opposite or ascetic principle," we shall be similarly inspired to say, "Quite correct, old bean," or "Got it the first time, old top," and merely propose an adjournment for convivial refreshment."[30]

The person who cultivates prayerfulness cannot help but also cultivate playfulness. For prayer nourishes union with the Divine Mystery Which (or Who) plays. It is therefore no accident that the first words in *The Gospel of Buddha* are "Rejoice at the glad tidings!"[31]

Chapter 3

The Art of Contemplative Prayer

Contemplation has been defined as "a long, loving look at the real." This applies to more than contemplative prayer. It embraces any activity that might be called contemplative. Contemplation can take many forms, from watching a wildflower sway gently in the sunshine to looking out a window at the falling rain; from gazing at a star-filled night sky to carefully pondering words read in a book. A father or mother gazing lovingly at a sleeping infant represents contemplation of the first order. Any "long, loving look at the real" can be contemplation. What turns contemplation into contemplative prayer and meditation is the conscious awareness of turning yourself toward the Divine Mystery, or God.

Thomas Merton drew on many religious traditions for spiritual wisdom. He is perhaps the best teacher of contemplative prayer for our time because he drew on traditions of both the West and the East; yet, as a Westerner himself he spoke in ways that Westerners can follow.

At the same time, Merton insisted that contemplative prayer cannot be taught by one person to another. "It can only be hinted at, suggested, pointed to, symbolized."[1] To Merton, contemplative prayer is "the experiential grasp of reality as *subjective,* not so much 'mine' (which would signify 'belonging to the external self') but 'myself' in existential mystery."[2] The goal of contemplative prayer, Merton said, is "the humble realization of our mysterious being as persons in whom God dwells, with infinite sweetness and inalienable power."[3]

Merton thought it important to say what contemplative prayer is *not.*[4] He wrote that contemplative prayer is not "mere inertia, a tendency to inactivity, to psychic peace." Contemplative prayer is not "trance or ecstasy, nor the hearing of sudden unutterable words, nor the imagination of lights." Neither is it "the emotional fire and sweetness that come with religious exaltation," nor "enthusiasm," nor "the sense of being 'seized' by an elemental force and swept into liberation by mystical frenzy."

No one, Merton said, should hope to find in contemplative prayer "an escape from conflict, from anguish or from doubt. Contemplative prayer is not a form of 'spiritual anesthesia.'" Contemplative prayer is "no pain killer." Nor does contemplative prayer lead to religious certainty. Instead, "the contemplative suffers the anguish of realizing that he *no longer knows what God is.* Rather, the one who learns to practice authentic contemplative prayer learns that "there is no 'what' that can be called God." Rather, God "is the 'Thou' before whom our inmost 'I' springs into awareness." The experience upon which contemplative prayer depends, Merton wrote, is the realization "that the love of God seeks us in every situation, and seeks our good."[5]

Although contemplative prayer, or meditation, is often thought of as the domain of Eastern religions, particularly Buddhism and Zen, there is a long tradition of contemplative prayer in both Catholicism and Eastern Orthodoxy.[6] Contemporary Judaism also reveals a widening interest in various forms of meditation and contemplative prayer. Jewish meditation authority Avram Davis comments that for Jews, "meditation is meant to transform us from a state of ignorance to a state of wisdom, from a state of bondage (be it psychological or personal) to a state of being free."[7]

The same may be said for Islam, although most Islamic resources originate with Sufi practitioners of contemplative prayer. "When all of earthly knowledge is forced through the sieve of contemplation," comment American Sufi teachers James Fadiman and Robert Frager, "the few grains that remain are 'the pure gold of Spiritual sustenance' that provides true nourishment."[8]

The closer all the great religious traditions draw to contemplative prayer, the closer they draw to one another. The more they leave speech behind and compare contemplative experience, the more they seem to have in common. The truth is that contemplative prayer can have a place in anyone's life, regardless of the religious tradition in which he or she is grounded.

Christian thinkers point out that the first commandment of Jesus is to love God with our whole being, and the second is to love our neighbors as if they were ourselves.[9] Thus, the love of God—spending actual time loving God for God's own sake—is foundational to a Christian life. Indeed, it is precisely the experience of divine love that enables one to exercise an active love for other people. This means that for Christians, loving God is a high priority, and this can only mean making time for some form of contemplative prayer. The Christian life requires giving loving attention to the God defined by Christianity as "love."[10] Indeed, there is in Christianity an objective ethical requirement to love God:

> Just as we must eat and think and play, or else we wither and die, and just as we must develop good relations with other human beings if we are to develop as persons, so also we cannot hope to become fully human unless we love God. We are essentially relational beings. We are stunted when our relational potentials are unfulfilled. We have a native desire for God, and our hearts will shrivel up unless they beat for God. Hence, in order to become fully who we are, we must be growing in love for God.[11]

It is basic to Christianity that the followers of Christ are to follow his example, and it is clear from the Gospels that Jesus spent time in deep prayer, what we call contemplative prayer. "He prayed, and in that prayer he united his mind and heart with God. Our love for God requires something similar."[12]

Basic to a Christian understanding of contemplative prayer is its openness to God's love. Christians do not love God first. Rather, they first try to be open to God's love, to receive and experience God's love. This is where Christian contemplative prayer begins. Subsequently, the experience of God's love leads to loving God in return.

LECTIO DIVINA: A CHRISTIAN CONTEMPLATIVE PRAYER

One of the most ancient Christian methods of contemplative prayer carries the Latin name *lectio divina*, "holy reading." This method of prayer is commonly called, simply, *lectio*.

Lectio divina offers a simple approach to contemplative prayer, one that anyone can practice, yet one that offers great potential for experiencing God's love and loving God in return. The basic method of *lectio* consists of sitting quietly with a copy of the Bible open on your lap. The idea is to read scripture slowly, allowing the words to enter not only your mind but also your heart. You might begin with one of the Psalms. Perhaps the first two verses of Psalm 103 touch your heart: "Bless the Lord, O my soul, and all that is within me, bless his holy name. Bless the Lord, O my soul, and do not forget all his benefits."

The idea with *lectio* is to read slowly until a line or passage strikes a chord in your heart. Reread the words that touch you until you have them memorized. Then close your eyes, breathe evenly and slowly, and repeat the words to yourself for as long as you like. If, at some point, you feel inclined to simply rest in silent awareness of God's presence, do that for as long as you want to.

Finally, open your eyes and begin reading slowly again until another phrase or verse touches your heart, and repeat the process. *Lectio* may last any length of time, but ten or fifteen minutes seems to be the minimum length of time for the experience to "work."

This is a basic description of *lectio divina*, but it is possible to break it down into even more basic components and to consider each one as a movement toward contemplative prayer. Father M. Basil Pennington, a Trappist monk, suggests that as a way of praying the scriptures, *lectio divina* has six parts, or movements, each with a Latin name. They are *lectio* (reading), *meditatio* (meditation), *oratio* (prayer), *contemplatio* (contemplation), *compassio* (compassion), and *operatio* (action).[13]

Lectio, the first movement in *lectio divina*, is a quiet opening of one's whole self to the Word of God in the written words of scripture. The idea is to allow the Word to nourish us spiritually and to read scripture for spiritual, not informational, purposes.

Meditatio, the second movement, simply means repeating words or phrases that touch us deeply as we read them. This is not a cognitive operation; don't try to analyze what you are reading. Rather, open yourself to the Word and try to let it sink deeper into your whole self. The ideal is to become one with the words you read.

Oratio, the third movement, occurs when we respond from the heart to the Divine Mystery, or God, present within us through the Word of scripture that we have read. The Word speaks to us in the scriptures, and we respond with whatever prayer we feel inclined to pray. This may be a very simple phrase, such as "Thank you, God," "Help me know your love, Lord," or a single word such as "Peace." Or it may be a "wordier" prayer that tells God of our concerns or joys.

Contemplatio, the fourth movement, cannot be

forced. It must happen naturally and by itself. At such moments, perhaps following the *oratio* movement, after our words of prayer have come to an end or we have gotten off our chest whatever we needed to get off our chest, then we are able to be quietly present to the One who is love and is always present within us. This awareness of the divine is a gift. It is not something we can force or make happen. It is not a reward for our efforts. Either it happens or it does not happen; sometimes it will, sometimes it won't.

Compassio, the fifth movement, is one of the consequences of *lectio divina.* It is an opening to and an awareness of the lack of wholeness that characterizes the world and everything in it, an acknowledgment of the fact of human suffering and the tragic nature of human existence itself. This is an experience of unity with God and with all people and all beings now alive. Again, this movement cannot be made to happen; either it happens or it doesn't, and usually we must practice *lectio* for some time before experiencing this movement.

Operatio, the sixth and final movement, is the perception that we are called to act on behalf of others. We perceive that God not only calls us to act but also gifts us with the grace and power we need to act on behalf of others to bring peace and healing.

Father Pennington summarizes the contemporary Christian understanding of *lectio divina* as a way of contemplative prayer:

> All those who regularly meet the Lord in *lectio* will go beyond all the thoughts and ideas and concepts, no matter how fascinating they are, and enter into a contemplative union with God in Christ. They will come to have the

mind and heart of Christ, which is a heart of self-giving love, ever ready to give itself totally for the salvation and well-being of the human family.[14]

This is one example of a Christian form of contemplative prayer. Numerous other forms exist that are or can become contemplative. They include the Jesus prayer, praying the rosary (a form of devotional prayer that focuses on key events in the life of Jesus and invokes the intercession of Mary, the mother of Jesus. Traditionally, the person praying counts the prayers using a rosary, a string of beads similar to those used by Buddhists but with a small crucifix attached), centering prayer (similar to *lectio divina*, but utilizing a sacred word as a focal point), and the Eastern Orthodox prayer of watchfulness (an advanced form of meditation involving control over one's inner thoughts and feelings during prayer).[15] In each case, the student of contemplative prayer will discover numerous similarities among Eastern and Western forms of contemplative prayer or meditation.

BUDDHIST MEDITATION: A ROAD TO PEACE

Buddhist meditation is different from *lectio* in that it does not make use of sacred writings or words as a springboard to deep meditation. Rather, Buddhist meditation is "a journey one takes to reach peace."[16] In Buddhism, as in Christianity, meditation is not an end in itself but a means to an end. Still, the journey to peace is a rewarding experience in itself for what we may learn about ourselves and for the inner healing that may occur.

In Buddhist meditation, you sit still and allow your mind to be restful, since the mind, as well as the body, needs rest. "A sound, clear, and rested mind is essential if we are to fully enjoy the many blessings that life offers us. Such a tranquil mind can be realized through meditation."[17]

Buddhist meditation instructors typically teach four different postures for meditation: sitting, walking, standing, and lying down. Most Buddhist meditation practitioners prefer sitting.

The place you choose for meditation is important. Preferably, it should be a quiet place where you will not be disturbed. This may be a corner of a room or, if it is possible, an entire small room.

The time at which you meditate is also important. The ideal is a time when you are rested, not distracted, and alert. For some people, this may be the first thing in the morning, upon waking. For others, it may be a bit later in the morning or in the evening.

Finally, there are always distractions during meditation, especially sounds you cannot control. Buddhist meditation teachers advise learning how not to resist distracting sounds. Rather, learn to observe how the sounds come and go, and observe how the mind reacts to the sounds. "Mastery of that aspect of meditation is a major step forward in your spiritual growth."[18]

One form of Buddhist meditation involves being aware of your breathing. This is called *anapana sati*.[19] The purpose of this is to refresh the mind, relieve stress, and discover inner peace. You may practice *anapana sati* almost anywhere: at home, riding a bus or train, during a formal meditation session, or at work. This form of meditation is most helpful, however, when you feel "stressed out" and distracted.

To practice *anapana sati,* first find a comfortable posture, then close your eyes and take a few deep breaths. At the beginning of your meditation, inhale and briefly hold your breath. When you exhale, release the breath slowly, being sure to empty your lungs of as much breath as possible. Do this several times. Once you have calmed down, allow your breathing to become normal and focus on your breath. Be aware of how the air feels as it passes in and out of your nostrils. Focus as completely as possible on your breathing as if nothing else mattered. Direct your attention to each breath and follow it as it comes and goes.

If distracting thoughts enter your mind, don't resist them. With great gentleness, simply bring your attention back to your breathing. As your focus on breathing deepens, you will be less distracted by thoughts or by occurrences around you. Be in the present moment, and be with your breathing for as long as you wish. Allow each breath to refresh your mind and relax you physically. When you are ready to finish your meditation, bring it gently to a close and open your eyes.

ZEN MEDITATION: CULTIVATING AN EMPTY MIND

In Zen Buddhism, contemplative prayer takes the form of prolonged daily periods of meditation, particularly meditation that Zen calls *zazen.* Zen Buddhism developed during the sixth century, and Zen meditation, like

Buddhist meditation in general, is seen as a means of liberation from suffering.[20] There are strict precepts you must follow in order to practice this form of contemplative prayer.

> A student of Tendai, a philosophical school of Buddhism, came to the Zen abode of Gasan as a pupil. When he was departing a few years later Gasan warned him: "Studying the truth speculatively is useful as a way of collecting preaching material. But remember that unless you meditate constantly your light of truth may go out."[21]

In order to understand the nature and purpose of *zazen*, it is necessary to have a basic grasp of Zen itself. The name *Zen* comes from a Sanskrit word, *dhyana*, which means "meditation." By practicing Zen meditation, the practitioner stills his or her thoughts and grows in awareness of the empty mind that usually contains thoughts. "Just as the particles in a glass of muddy water settle to the bottom when the glass is no longer shaken and the water becomes transparent, so thoughts settle down when the mind is not agitated and consciousness becomes clear."[22]

Zen itself, however, is not meditation. Zen is a way of life, a way of being-in-the-world. The goal of Zen is not to become a champion, world-class meditator, one who meditates almost endlessly. Rather, the "goal" of Zen is "no-goal." Zen is a new spiritual self, which is "no-self." The teachings of Zen frequently seem paradoxical, but the purpose of Zen—which is "no-purpose"—is to transcend apparent paradoxes.

Zen teaches that we are not the transitory mortals we take ourselves to be. We are eternal Buddha-nature. Anything the mind thinks itself to be is just a thought in the mind. It is an illusion. Buddha-nature is the mind itself. The idea of who we are is a false self—our ego. It is like a cloud that obscures the empty sky of our essential Buddha-nature, that is our true identity. In the absence of this idea, we know ourselves to be the empty void of pure consciousness. We understand that all things, including our separate identities, are animated by one mind, and we are that. This is enlightenment.[23]

The "enlightenment" that Zen meditation seeks is "to penetrate the nature of things to attain the buddha-nature," to use a traditional Zen phrase. *Satori* (enlightenment) means becoming what we already are. *Zazen* is a discipline meant to lead to *satori*. There is no sense in Buddhism or Zen of a personal God as understood by Judaism, Christianity, and Islam. Rather, there is only the Buddha-nature which underlies all appearances. At the same time, it is worth noting that "personal God" is a metaphor that stands for the absolute Divine Mystery Which/Who transcends all concepts.

The practice of *zazen* is not complicated, but it is also not easy. *Zazen* is usually done sitting on a cushion with the back straight and the legs crossed. The right hand is held about two inches below the navel with the palm upward. The left hand rests in the right, also palm upward, and the ends of the thumbs are touching. The *zazen* practitioner keeps the eyes half closed, the gaze relaxed, looking at nothing in particular. During the practice of *zazen*, the attention is located just below the navel, an area called the *hara*, which helps to relax the body and steady the mind. This makes it easier to stop the confusion of thoughts. Ancient Zen masters taught that one should sit during *zazen* "with noble strength like a great pine tree or an iron mountain."[24]

During Zen meditation, particularly as a beginner, you silently count according to your breathing, with one count given to each breath that is inhaled and exhaled. Thus: inhale, exhale, one; inhale, exhale, two; inhale, exhale, three. . . . The goal of this discipline is to get the mind to settle down. This may take several years of *zazen* to accomplish. More advanced *zazen* practitioners remain aware of their breathing without counting. In *zazen*, your breathing pattern is always allowed to continue according to its natural rhythm, but over time breathing becomes slower, deeper, and more regular.

The most advanced, and most difficult, form of *zazen* is called *shikan-taza*. This consists of sitting without any focus of concentration, sometimes imagining yourself to be in a 360-degree sphere of awareness.[25] Even this image must, however, be abandoned. "*Shikan-taza* is often compared to the alertness of someone involved in a life or death sword fight. Most important is to sit in the faith that this 'just sitting' can and does naturally unfold to total self-realization, called Buddhahood."[26]

Closely related to *zazen* is the use of *koans*, questions that seem absurd. One of the most famous *koans* is "What is the sound of one hand clapping?" But the ultimate *koans* are "Who am I?" and "What is the absolute?" Zen teaches that there are three essential qualities necessary in order to resolve the *koan*: great faith, great determination, and great doubt.[27] The purpose of *koans* is to help one attain *satori* by transcending the false self.

> A student asked, "What is Zen?" The master answered, "It is right before your eyes." The student asked, "So why can't I see it?" The master answered, "Because you have a 'me.'" The student asked, "If I no longer have the concept 'me,' will I realize Zen?" The master answered, "If there is no 'me' who wants to realize Zen?"[28]

Much in Buddhist and Zen forms of meditation is perfectly compatible with Jewish, Christian, and Islamic/ Sufi forms of contemplative prayer. Once again, Thomas Merton is the best-known example of someone who adapted Zen meditation techniques to his practice of contemplative prayer as a Catholic monk. Some mainline— that is, non-fundamentalist/evangelical—Christians learn to use Buddhist and Zen meditation techniques in their practice of contemplative prayer. Likewise for some Jews and Muslims. On a cognitive level, for *satori* they simply substitute union with the Divine Mystery Christians know as loving Father, Judaism calls the Lord God, or Muslims/Sufis know by numerous names such as the All-Compassionate One. Such Jewish, Christian, or Muslim/Sufi practitioners of Buddhist or Zen meditation often observe, in dialogue with Buddhists and Zen Buddhists, that on the level of contemplative experience there is little if any difference between them and that the main difference occurs on the cognitive, not the experiential, level.

SUFISM: LOVING GOD

Beginning in the 700s, within Islam there arose a more mystical tradition called Sufism, which emphasized the inner spiritual state of love and devotion to God. Many different Sufi groups came into being, some of which survive to this day. Sufism uses music, drumming, and dance in its worship. In Turkey, the Mevlevi order, widely known as the Whirling Dervishes, practiced a dance meant to symbolize the planets whirling around the sun. In recent decades, Sufism has undergone extensive growth, even in the United States.

From the Sufi tradition we can learn the most about Islamic contemplative prayer.[29] This is so because "Sufism is a mystical path of love in which God, or Truth, is experienced as the Beloved. The inner relationship of lover and Beloved is the core of the Sufi path."[30] Images of love, beloved, and lover return to this discussion because with Islam we return to a personal God. Yet, when the Sufi says that "We have come from God and we return to God,"[31] this sounds remarkably similar to the Buddhist concept that we already are what we seek to become.

Sounding similar to both Buddhist and Zen meditation, as well as various Christian forms of contemplative prayer, the Sufi meditation teacher declares that "the greatest obstacle that keeps us from experiencing this eternal state of union is the ego, our own personal identity. In the state of union, there is no ego. In this moment, the individual self ceases to exist and only the Beloved [i.e., God] exists."[32]

Different Sufi groups use different methods of meditation. One method, called the meditation of the heart, uses the energy of love to go beyond the mind.[33] The idea is to give yourself entirely to God in love during the meditation time. "When we give ourself in love to the Beloved this experience is amplified many times, which is why Sufis are often referred to as 'Idiots of God.' In the words of [the Sufi mystic] 'Attâr, 'When love comes, reason disappears. Reason cannot live with the folly of love; love has nothing to do with human reason.'"[34]

During the meditation of the heart, the meditator imagines three things:

1. Imagine that you go deeper and deeper into your inmost self. There you will find the very center of yourself, where there is peace, stillness, and above all love. For God is Love, and you are all love, since you are made in God's image. But you have forgotten this. Deep in your heart you can rediscover this love.

2. After you find this place deep within, imagine that you are seated there surrounded by the love of God. Here you are in deep peace, sheltered, secure, loved by God, and there is no outside self; the inner self is all. Your whole being is sheltered in the love of God.

3. As you continue sitting in meditation, at peace in God's presence, distracting thoughts may enter your mind. Imagine that you drown all thoughts and images and feelings in the feeling of love. If you do this meditation well, all distracting thoughts will disappear and your mind will remain empty. Love will be all.[35]

One main purpose of Sufi meditation is to cultivate a center of stillness and love in the midst of the knock-about world with its difficulties and limitations. The Sufi does not reject the world and creation but strives to know its deeper purpose as a reflection of God's

Oneness. "The way of the Sufi is to contain duality within the oneness of love."[36]

JEWISH CONTEMPLATIVE PRAYER: CONVERSING WITH GOD

Judaism, too, has a mystical tradition that teaches contemplative forms of prayer. Prayer is an essential part of any Jewish life, but in this case prayer refers more to the daily recitation of prayers and blessings. It is not the same as contemplative prayer or meditation. At the same time, at least one rabbi insists that all prayer has the potential for true spiritual depth: "To pray with true sincerity, to reach spiritual heights as a result of true prayer, is not easy. It requires training and practice. It is an art itself."[37]

The heart of what we might call the Jewish contemplative or mystical tradition is Kabbalah, a Hebrew word that means "receiving" or "that which has been received." Kabbalah has a twofold meaning. It refers first to tradition, to ancient wisdom passed down and now treasured from the past. Kabbalah also refers to the fact that if we are truly receptive, wisdom arrives spontaneously and takes us by surprise.[38]

As with all the great spiritual traditions, Kabbalah cannot simply be taught by one person to another. Rather, it must also be experienced. "And while its metaphors and history make it a uniquely 'Jewish' form of spiritual practice, the kabbalistic experience is universal in that it aims to realize the 'No-thingness' of all things."[39]

The practice of Kabbalistic meditation takes many

forms, structured and unstructured. Regardless of the specific method, however, the focus of meditation is the God of Israel who is a personal God.

For those of a devotional inclination, there is the Hasidic informal conversation with God.

One focused meditation practice is called *gerushin*— a method similar to *lectio divina* in that it takes a biblical verse as a subject for contemplation. Visually inclined people may choose to concentrate on a candle flame, a flower, or a picture. The idea is to let the essence of the object lead you to experience No-thingness. Others may wish to use the verbal repetition of prayers or other words or phrases to focus the mind.

More psychological meditation methods allow us to work with positive and negative feelings or emotions, such as love and anger. The most difficult form of meditation, sometimes called nondirected meditation, focuses directly on No-thingness.

Frequently—and Kabbalistic meditation is a good example—contemplative forms of prayer and meditation from the various religious traditions sound similar to one another. Notice how the following words from Kabbalah sound remarkably similar to words a Buddhist or Hindu might speak:

> The depth of primordial being is called Boundless. Because of its concealment from all creatures above and below, it is also called Nothingness. If one asks, "What is it?" the answer is, "Nothing," meaning: No one can understand anything about it. It is negated of every conception. No one can know anything about it—except the belief that it exists. Its existence cannot be grasped by anyone

other than it. Therefore its name is "I am becoming."[40]

Isaac Luria (1543–1620), who was an early Kabbalist and Jewish mystical teacher called "the Ari" ("the Lion"), characterized Jewish meditation as *kavvanah*, "concentrated awareness." He also wrote instructions for the Kabbalist to follow in daily prayers. Luria described deepening stages of concentration, including *hitbonenut*, in which the meditator contemplates creation until he or she is indistinguishable from it, and *hitbodedut*, exterior and interior seclusion from the world and from thought. The goal of *hitbonenut* is to gaze at an object without thinking about it. This non-thinking would gradually bring the Kabbalist to "an experience of the interpenetration of absolute and relative worlds."[41]

The great twentieth-century Kabbalist and teacher Rabbi Abraham Isaac Kook instructed his students to "increase aloneness" [*hitbodedut*] and—sounding much like a Zen *koan*—penetrate the question "What are we?" thus to find bliss, transcending all humiliations or anything that happens, by attaining equanimity, by becoming one with everything that happens, by reducing yourself so extremely that you nullify your individual, imaginary form, that you nullify existence in the depth of your self. For with the realization that the self is "Nothing" comes "the light of peace. . . . The desire to act and work, the passion to create and restore yourself, the yearning for silence and for the inner shout of joy—these all bond together in your spirit, and you become holy."[42]

As similar as this may appear to be to Eastern mysticism, it is clear that Kabbalah and its meditation techniques are rooted in the experience of a personal God. "The intimate relationship between God and the devotional spiritual seeker is the basis for all meditative prayer."[43] At the same time, Jewish mysticism insists that because there are limits to the human intellect, those who meditate must reach a point in their experience where they follow faith alone. Ultimately, it is the first commandment—to love God—that motivates the seeker. Yet, paradoxically, this experience of "No-thingness" is an experience of the God who is immanent, not transcendent.

> Depending on the seeker's preference, the immanent God could be visualized as either male or female, father or mother, lover or friend. From these relationships emerged the symbolism of the Divine Marriage and the Mystic Bride and Bridegroom that later appeared in the writings of Christian mystics. Such meditations allowed feelings to flow freely as the meditator, with eyes closed, was immersed in a world blazing with color and dancing with light.[44]

The meditation techniques associated with Kabbalah require an awareness of a rather esoteric "map" used to chart the Kabbalist's contemplative journey. Using this "map," the Kabbalist finds access to the unknowable God. This "map" takes the form of a staff with six "branches," three on either side of the staff, each one representing a *sefirah* (plural: *sefirot*), which can be translated as spheres, worlds, emanations, or stages of consciousness.[45] For our purposes, it is not necessary to go into detail about this map. It is sufficient to know that the *sefirot* include such qualities as Understanding, Knowledge, Beauty, and Mercy.

Kabbalistic meditation techniques include that of

gazing. You might gaze at your own hand, for example, while repeating the Hebrew word *Gevurah*, which represents the *sefirah* of Power. Or, you might gaze at the flame of a candle and contemplate the five colors in the flame: white, green, red, black, and sky blue. Each color represents a *sefirah*. Continual gazing at the flame or some other appropriate object produces an "aura" of the object, which in turn can lead to the mental quiet needed for *hitbonenut* (consciousness of your unity with creation) to take place.

In another form of meditation, the Kabbalist gazes at the letters of the Holy Name (YHVH) and relates them in a visualization with the goal of unifying the male and female aspects of himself or herself.[46] Yet another form of meditation involves gazing into water in order to quiet your mind. This technique is based on a story in the Book of Ezekiel in which the prophet Ezekiel experiences self-realization upon gazing into the river Kvar, whose name means "already." This symbolizes yet another insight that sounds much like an idea in Zen meditation: that what you are seeking you already have—self-realization and union with God.

Yet another form of Kabbalistic meditation is called letter meditation. The Book of Genesis says that God created the world by the power of the word. "Hence, since the three primordial [Hebrew] letters of Creation (*Alef*/Air; *Mem*/Water; *Shin*/Fire) contain the elements connected with the breath, and thus with the generative power of the Word, in both their potential and manifest forms, they channel the energy sustaining the universe."[47]

Because human beings also are made up of these same elements, meditating on these Hebrew letters is a way to unite yourself with the whole of Creation. Here letters are used as a way to experience pure being, not as a way to communicate. As an alternative, Kabbalists may meditate on the letters in the sacred name of God (YHVH), with no reference to the male and female aspects of the self as in the method described above. The great medieval Kabbalist Isaac of Akko instructed his disciples to "place in front of the eyes of your mind the letters of God's name, as if they were written in a book in Hebrew script. Visualize every letter extending to infinity. . . . When you visualize the letters, focus on them with your mind's eye as you contemplate infinity. Both together: gazing and meditating."[48]

Some authorities on Kabbalah emphasize the importance of learning as much as possible about Kabbalah before trying to apply its disciplines to the practice of meditation.[49] It is no good, most meditators insist, to rush into meditation hoping for miracles or hoping for a magic cure for all of your personal and spiritual problems.

Jewish meditation supports a commitment to living a good, or righteous, life. You do this not merely by studying Torah but by *becoming* Torah. And this is done by living the commandments in your daily life.

Jewish meditation has a creative and devotional stage, which includes affective feelings for God. This stage keeps meditation from becoming dry and abstract. It is important to spend time each day in meditation. The goal is to integrate the results, or "fruits," of meditation into your ordinary, everyday life.

Contemporary Jewish spiritual guides emphasize the importance of enlisting the services of a qualified teacher and practicing meditation with a like-minded group—advice that might well apply to contemplative prayer in any tradition. "Aspiring Kabbalists must search around, attend workshops, study groups, and seminars, and make inquiries until they find a community suited to their individual needs and temperaments."[50]

Contemplative prayer requires cultivating the ability to quiet down, focus, and remain oriented toward the divine in the depths of oneself. In an era ruled by cultural superficiality, if we hope to live with any depth at all, meditation becomes a virtual necessity. We must take at least a few minutes each day to sit still, be quiet, be open, and listen with the ears of the heart to what we may hear. "Though it may sound strange to modern ears, we should without shame enroll as apprentices in the school of contemplative prayer."[51]

These insights from several religious traditions may be adapted for your own practice of contemplative prayer and used according to the religious tradition to which you belong. It is important to recall that the best way to benefit from various traditions is from within one particular tradition. To recall the words of Sri Swami Satchidananda: "I don't recommend trying to walk on all the different paths at once because you will never reach your goal that way."[52]

Chapter 4

The Importance of Solitude and Silence

I find that *people who think too much* are also often—consciously or unconsciously—people who are starving for lack of solitude and silence in their lives. One of the great ironies of our time is that one of the most basic conditions for an authentic spiritual life is a condition that most people avoid. Without silence and solitude, the human spirit shrivels up or goes into hiding out of a sheer instinct to survive. As Thomas Merton wrote from his perspective as a Catholic monk: "The ears with which one hears the message of the Gospel are hidden in man's heart, and these ears do not hear anything unless they are favored with a certain interior solitude and silence."[1]

Solitude and silence are necessary for each person to be genuinely free, and they are necessary if we are to have even the chance to cultivate the life of the spirit, to engage in some form of daily prayer and meditation, and to enjoy authentic relationships with other people. This is so because only in silence and solitude can we discover our true selves, as opposed to the egocentric self. Only in this way do we have a chance to see the light of day.

There is a kind of priority, here. First comes solitude, then silence, then prayer. The religious person enters into solitude in order to experience silence and be silent himself or herself. Then silence gives birth to prayer in the heart. So solitude and silence are cultivated for the sake of prayer. But there is a kind of ongoing cycle, for prayer enriches and deepens the experience of solitude and silence, which again lead to prayer.

Notice, too, that each part of solitude-silence-prayer requires a conscious choice. We must choose to be alone. We must choose to be silent. And we must choose to use solitude and silence for prayer and meditation. Thus, solitude and silence become pregnant and give birth to the divine, but not without our conscious cooperation.

The main problem for people today is that the dominant culture in which they live is based on unreality. As Merton wrote: "There is no greater disaster in the spiritual life than to be immersed in unreality, for life is maintained and nourished in us by our vital relation with realities outside and above us. When our life feeds on unreality, it must starve. It must therefore die."[2]

Our culture is dominated in large part by electronic media, which are largely controlled by the entertainment industry, which is largely controlled by international corporations, which are run by people whose primary values are material, not human and spiritual. This is so because the values of the audience—meaning us—are primarily material, not spiritual. Consequently, the dominant culture encourages behavior that supports values that are superficial, illusory, and not infrequently violent. In other words, countless millions of people's lives "feed on unreality." The only alternative is a life that makes the special effort needed to cultivate, to one degree or another, some objectivity with regard to the dominant culture, some mental and spiritual distance from it. This, in turn, depends on one's willingness and ability to spend time in solitude and silence—not solitude and silence for their own sake, but *prayerful* solitude and silence. The idea is to make room in our life to cultivate the life of the spirit and of the deeper self, where the Divine Mystery dwells.

Prior to the modern industrial and technological era, which began in the nineteenth century, most people lived a rural existence. Not to romanticize that era, but in those days the average life was quieter, the average day was less hectic, and the average person lived closer to the natural world, for good and for ill. People were not pummeled by commercial messages for several hours a day. For all the hard work required simply to survive from one day to the next, life presented people with regular opportunities to be alone, to reflect, to listen to the murmurings of their own hearts. Today, life in the so-called developed nations is so permeated by unreality that countless millions of people spend their entire lives alienated from their own deepest selves, thinking that what they need to be happy can be bought, if only they had enough money.

Even our homes are invaded daily by the dominant culture of unreality—in particular television, video movies, and the Internet. We fill our homes so much with electronic media that the average home is more an entertainment center than a place for human intimacy. Complete freedom from the effects of this culture is virtually impossible. Even monasteries are connected to this culture, so people who live there cannot claim a superior aloofness. All the same, those who recognize the true state of affairs and want to cultivate an authentic human and spiritual life have no choice but to do whatever is necessary to find regular experiences of solitude and silence where they can be prayerful and open to the Divine Mystery. This is as true for those who are married and are parents as it is for those who are single; as true for people who live in families or other small social groups as for those who live alone. Regular experiences of prayerful solitude and silence are necessary if we are to preserve our humanity.

Christians point to the example of Jesus, who according to the Gospels frequently went off to be alone with God in prayer. "In the morning, while it was still very dark, he got up and went out to a deserted place, and there he prayed" (Mark 1:35). Indeed, the entire, vast tradition of Christian mysticism and contemplative prayer presupposes the need for solitude and silence.

"SILENCE IS THE NATURE OF GOD"

Perhaps the best philosophy of silence written from a Western perspective appears in a book originally published three years after the end of World War II. The author of *The World of Silence* was Max Picard. Picard, a physician, had become disillusioned with the modern practice of medicine, which seemed to overlook the humanity of the patient. So he left the large hospital where he was practicing, began to study philosophy, and eventually moved to a remote village, where he reflected on modern life.

In *The World of Silence*, Max Picard declares that silence is independent of the existence of anything else. Silence does not depend on anything else in order to be. Silence is always there, even when it is covered over by a wall of sound. Silence is not the same thing as the absence of sounds. Silence is "an autonomous phenomenon."[3]

> Silence is nothing merely negative; it is not the mere absence of speech. It is a positive, a complete world in itself.
>
> Silence has greatness simply because it is. It *is*, and that is its greatness, its pure existence.
>
> There is no beginning to silence and no end: it seems to have its origins in the time when everything was still pure Being. It is like uncreated, everlasting Being.
>
> When silence is present, it is as though nothing but silence had ever existed. . . .
>
> We cannot imagine a world in which there is nothing but language and speech, but we can imagine a world where there is nothing but silence. . . .
>
> Silence is the only phenomenon today that is "useless." It does not fit into the world of profit and utility; it simply *is*. It seems to have no other purpose; it cannot be exploited.[4]

Picard spoke of the "holy uselessness" of silence because silence points to "a state where only being is valid: the state of the Divine." In fact, he declares, "The mark of the

Divine in things is preserved by their connection with the world of silence."[5]

This is why silence is so vitally important to this discussion. Only by making room in our life for periods of prayerful silence can we preserve in ourselves "the mark of the Divine." For, Picard says, silence is the only reality that "cannot be traced back to anything else."[6] There is nothing "behind" silence to which it can be related except the Divine Mystery, God, "the Creator Himself."[7] Indeed, "sometimes all the noise of the world today seems like the mere buzzing of insects on the broad back of silence."[8]

Human beings, Max Picard said, need a substance of silence within themselves; otherwise, they will be unable to cope with a world filled with sound, much of it mere noise. Indeed, human happiness depends on the cultivation of an inner substance of silence. "There is an immeasurability in happiness that only feels at home in the breadth of silence. Happiness and silence belong together just as do profit and noise."[9]

Genuine words, words worth listening to, Picard says, must arise from time spent in prayerful silence. If we are to benefit from hearing these words, they must fall on ears that listen with ears opened by time spent in silence. "Instead of truly speaking to others today we are all waiting merely to unload on to others the words that have collected inside us. Speech has become a purely animal, excretive function."[10]

Writing just before television became a mass medium, Picard discussed radio in ways that have clear implications for television, as well. In particular, his observations address the environment we cultivate in our homes:

Radio is a machine producing absolute verbal noise. The content hardly matters anymore. . . .

Radio has occupied the whole space of silence. There is no silence any longer. Even when the radio is turned off the radio-noise still seems to go on inaudibly. Radio-noise is so amorphous that it seems to have no beginning and no end; it is limitless. And the type of man formed by the constant influence of this noise is the same: formless, undecided inwardly and externally, with no definite limits and standards. . . .

There is no longer any space in which it is possible to be silent, for space has all been occupied now in advance. . . .

There is no more silence, only intervals between radio-noises.[11]

In the final chapter, "Silence and Faith," of Picard's book, he explains the relationship between silence and our relationship with the Divine Mystery. Silence, Picard says, is the natural basis for cultivating intimacy with the divine. Here we have, in a cosmic nutshell, the reason why silence is so crucial to the cultivation of spiritual vitality: "It is a sign of the love of God that a mystery is always separated from man by a layer of silence. And that is a reminder that man should also keep a silence in which to approach the mystery."[12]

Picard insists that through silence we encounter the Divine Mystery, or God, in ways not possible under any other condition. It is "in silence that that first meeting between man and the Mystery of God is accomplished."[13] And it is in silence that words come into the human heart that are worth speaking; "from silence the word also receives the power to become extraordinary as the Mystery of God is extraordinary."[14]

Silence is the necessary foundation for a vital, authentic spirituality because "just as language constitutes the nature of man, so silence is the nature of God."[15]

Max Picard makes the critical connection between prayer and silence. He explains: "In prayer the region of the lower, human silence comes into relation with the higher silence of God; the lower rests in the higher."[16]

Finally, Picard concludes his book with a quotation from the early nineteenth-century Danish philosopher Søren Kierkegaard: words that say clearly why silence is so vitally important in our time, words that must have been especially powerful for Picard, who left the practice of medicine because he saw illnesses in society that conventional medicine could do nothing about. He quotes Kierkegaard:

> The present state of the world and of the whole of life is diseased. If I were a doctor and were asked for my advice, I should reply: Create silence! Bring men to silence. The Word of God cannot be heard in the noisy world of today. And even if it were blazoned forth with all the panoply of noise so that it could be heard in the midst of all the other noise, then it would no longer be the word of God. Therefore create silence.[17]

Meeting Ourselves in Solitude

Silence is as close as anyone can get to the transcendence of the Divine Mystery. Once the modern person is able to calm down, sit down, and sit still, silence has a healing effect on the person that nothing else can accomplish. To be in silence is to make possible the life of the spirit, the life of the deepest self—and prayer itself.

Of course, this is where the two topics of this chapter come together, for it is in solitude that we are most likely to encounter the mystery of silence. Virtually every major religious tradition takes for granted the value of silence and solitude. For without true interior solitude, external solitude is of little value. Learning to be alone, to encounter your true self in union with the Divine Mystery, is the ultimate purpose of solitude. The paradox of solitude, however, is that we should spend time in solitude so we can cultivate an interior solitude that is always there, whether or not we are in solitude.

> To love solitude and to seek it does not mean constantly traveling from one geographical possibility to another. A man becomes a solitary at the moment when, no matter what may be his external surroundings, he is suddenly aware of his own inalienable solitude and sees that he will never be anything but solitary. From that moment, solitude is not potential—it is actual.[18]

One of the greatest obstacles to an authentic spiritual life in our time is the reluctance many people have to admit their own ultimate solitude. We come into the world alone when we are born, and we leave the world alone when we die. Yet, many people spend their entire lives trying to escape from this fact. One of the dangerous aspects of modern mass culture is the extent to which it alienates people from their own ultimate solitude by encouraging a kind of herd mentality and the idea that we can't possibly be happy unless we are with other people. This then translates into the assumption that we must be accepted by others to be happy, which in turn translates into the belief that we must measure up to other people's expectations in order to be happy.

Every religion that makes room for a mystical spirituality, or for a contemplative dimension—which includes virtually every religion except fundamentalist/evangelical forms of Christianity—takes for granted the importance of solitude and silence as part of a whole and healthy life.

Rebbe Nachman of Breslov (1772–1810), one of the most widely respected Hasidic Jewish spiritual masters, said: "Make it a daily habit to seclude yourself in *hitbodedut*—meditation. Express your innermost thoughts and feelings before God each day in the language you are most comfortable with."[19]

Indeed, the Jewish tradition of keeping the Sabbath presupposes that on that day each person will spend some time alone, in prayer, and in reading Torah. "The study of Torah should constitute one of the leisure activities that one pursues on the Sabbath."[20] While there are plenty of family and community rituals and activities on the Sabbath, this island of holy leisure that crowns each week also includes time for each person to be alone.

The example set by the founder of a religion invariably has a profound impact on the subsequent history of that religion. The experience of the Buddha, for example, and the fact that he experienced enlightenment while sitting in solitude under the bodhi tree, means that his followers ever since have placed a high value on solitary meditation. The same is true of Hinduism. While meditation requires time alone, it is understood that solitude is not an end in itself but a means to greater union with the Divine Mystery. Both silence and solitude are undertaken for the sake of a deeper prayer life or deeper meditation.

Catholicism and Eastern Orthodoxy also have an explicit tradition of reflecting about solitude and silence. These ancient forms of Christianity understand silence to mean that you stop talking so you can pray and reflect better and give greater attention to God. The assumption here is that while we are present to other people in a distinctively human fashion through speaking, speech can easily become an expression of flight from ourselves, from others, and from God. Talking can be a mere diversion, a waste of time; indeed, everyone has met people who seem to be compulsive talkers. This category of speech would also include gossiping, the constant babble of the mass media, and commercial and political propaganda. Therefore, to make room in our day for silence is a counter-cultural move.

The seriously devoted person's prayer and spirituality make a difference in how he or she lives in the ordinary, everyday world. A contemporary American Zen Buddhist authority says:

> At the heart of our practice, behind everything
> else, surrounding everything else, within

everything else—such spatial metaphors are
inevitably inadequate—is silence. We have little experience of silence in our world today,
and the culture as a whole seems to value only
more and more elaborate kinds of sound. Yet
our sitting practice is silent, and retreats are
profoundly so. Enlightenment has been called
the great silence. In that way, Buddhist practice is at odds with the culture. It is at odds
with every culture.[21]

The genuinely prayerful person seeks times of silence
not because speaking is bad but because true speech is
nourished by silence. The same may be said about solitude. We enter into prayerful solitude not to avoid other
people but to cultivate greater union with the Divine
Mystery and to nourish, at the same time, deeper, health-
ier, more fruitful relationships with others. The need for
solitude is clear, for example, in the Buddha's description of how the disciple should practice meditation. The
first requirement is solitude: "He chooses some lonely
spot to rest at."[22]

In ancient Christian tradition, the primary purpose
of solitude is to be alone with God, and nothing could be
further from loneliness. As Carol Frances Jegen writes,
"Genuine solitude is rooted in each person's uniqueness.
In limitless love God created each human person with a
possibility of sharing divine life in a personal way that
can never be duplicated."[23]

We need to be realistic, however. In modern technological societies it can be difficult to find solitude and
silence. "The rapid pace of life, the urbanization process
with its crowded living conditions, and the constant
communication provided by the media often present

almost insurmountable difficulties to [those] longing for periods of solitude in some regular patterns."[24]

At the same time, opportunities for solitude are not impossible to find. In or near virtually any urban center are retreat facilities that offer solitude to anyone who wishes to visit. In any given area, there are monasteries belonging to various religious traditions, and almost always they welcome visitors. Even in our own homes, we can find solitude and silence by simply staying home now and then and turning off the television, the stereo, and the radio. Even in families with young children, it is possible to find times for solitude and silence. Spouses can support each other in this by giving each other time away for solitude and silence: one shoulders parenting responsibilities while the other parent is away. Or a single parent can pair up with another single parent, one caring for the other's children while he or she is off for a silent retreat.

RUNNING TOWARD OURSELVES

If we place a high value on using our time in a particular way, we will make time to do it. If times of silence and solitude are important to us, we will make time for silence and solitude. Ultimately, however, we are not talking about silence and solitude for the sake of relieving stress, although they may do that. Rather, the ideal is to seek prayerful silence that nourishes interior spiritual silence. That silence will nourish our union with the Divine Mystery and thus our basic spiritual and human freedom.

In modern life, language is all around us: talking,

reading, writing, thinking, imagining. The media bombard us with words.

Modern life also has much to do with *doing*—with moving around, making things happen, building. An important, influential person is sometimes called a mover and shaker. But one purpose of prayerful solitude and silence is to renew our union with the truth that, in the long run, all human effort is without effect unless it is done in union with the Divine Mystery. "Unless the Lord builds the house," sings the Psalmist in the Hebrew Scriptures, "those who build it labor in vain. Unless the Lord guards the city, the guard keeps watch in vain."[25]

We live in a world that is flooded with words, where we are expected to be active, and productive—if we aren't, then our value decreases accordingly. Also, while possessing the most sophisticated communications technologies in the history of the world, many people find it difficult to communicate with the most important people in their lives—their own families. All our words, all our busy-ness, all our technology—none of this has given us peace, inner happiness, or joy. We still find it difficult to live together with one another in peace.

Despite our many words and activities, inside we are poverty-stricken. Spiritually, we are destitute. One major reason is that each person is far from being at peace with himself or herself. And one of the main reasons is that we are alienated from our own deepest center, which can be found only in prayerful silence and solitude. Because we run away from ourselves all the time, escaping into our activities and our technologies and our words, we never get in touch with our deepest self, and never with the divine at the center of our being. This makes it virtually impossible to communicate in any but a superficial fashion with other people, even those with whom we live most closely. Silence and solitude constitute the ultimate reality, and as long as we avoid them we thrash about on the surface of life.

As long as there is no place in our homes for prayerful silence in solitude, because we fill them with television and stereos and the like, we will remain on the surface of life. As long as there is no time in our week for solitary, silent prayer and meditation; as long as there is no place in each month for a day spent entirely alone in a silent place, say a retreat facility or a house of prayer; as long as there is no room in our life for prayerful solitude and silence; our work will be frantic and our relationships with one another will remain superficial and unsatisfying.

Sacrifices must be made to make room for prayerful silence and solitude. We must be willing to give up our former way of life and to accept the truth of our mortality, a source of spiritual power and freedom rarely faced except in solitude. We must be willing, as was the Buddha, to look directly and without flinching at the old man, the sick man, and the dead man, and accept the fact that this man is none other than us. Given this fact, each of us must ask: How am I going to live my days?

In prayerful solitude and silence, we can face and respond to the most basic of questions: Where did I come from? What am I doing here? Where am I going? The responses we give to such questions determine how we live our everyday life, and the answers can come only by spending time regularly in prayerful solitude and silence. For solitude and silence are anything but empty. Rather, nothing has more to teach us than silence, and nothing has more fullness than solitude. Silence "is actually a highly charged state, full of life. It couldn't be more alive. The energy in it is subtle and refined but extremely powerful."[26]

It should be clear by now that solitude is not the same as loneliness. Loneliness can, however, lead to an awareness of our inalienable solitude and union with the Divine Mystery. A twentieth-century Protestant theologian, Paul Tillich, once wrote of an instance when loneliness led to solitude for him:

> I never felt so lonely as in that particular hour when I was surrounded by people but suddenly realized my ultimate isolation. I became silent and retired from the group in order to be alone with my loneliness. I wanted my external predicament to match my internal one.
>
> Loneliness can be compared only by those who can bear solitude. We have a natural desire for solitude because we are men. We want to feel what we are—namely, alone—not in pain and horror, but with joy and courage. There are many ways in which solitude can be sought and experienced. And each way can be called "religious," if it is true, as one philosopher said, that "religion is what man does with his solitariness."[27]

As mentioned above, the purpose of exterior silence and solitude is to nourish interior silence and solitude. The primary way to do this is not simply to go into a silent, solitary place and sit there, perhaps reading a book. To be sure, in a noisy world it is healthy to be alone and quiet. But in order for solitude and silence to have a chance in the depths of one's being, it is necessary to practice some form of contemplative prayer or meditation, as discussed in the previous chapter. Indeed, the goal of contemplative prayer is precisely this deep inner silence, allowing this deep silence to struggle to the surface of our inner being and, as it were, see the light of day.

BE ALERT AS IF YOUR LIFE DEPENDED ON IT

The main obstacle to experiencing the silence at the core of our being, of course, is noise—the noise that fills our inner self constantly, even when we sleep. "Most people discover that they cannot stop thinking for even one minute at a time," writes Rabbi David A. Cooper, an authority on contemporary Jewish mysticism. "We are not the rulers of our own minds! This is a depressing experience for some people. Thoughts come and go on their own, and there seems to be *nothing* we can do about it."[28]

Rabbi Cooper believes that it is not the task of meditation techniques to teach us how to get rid of these unruly thoughts. He tells a story of the great Hasidic master, the Baal Shem Tov, whose students heard that a renowned teacher would soon come to their town. The students wanted to know how they could tell whether this man was indeed a great teacher. "Ask him to advise you on what to do to keep unholy thoughts from disturbing your prayers and your studies," the Baal Shem Tov replied. "If this teacher gives you advice, you will know that he is not worthy. For it is the service of every person to struggle every hour until their death with extraneous thoughts, and time after time to uplift these thoughts and bring them into harmony with the nature of creation."[29]

Rabbi Cooper explains that it is not the purpose of Jewish contemplative practices to reach a prayerful state where no thoughts come into our minds. Rather, the goal is to "deal quickly and appropriately with whatever comes up, whether they are situations with other people, or thoughts in our minds."[30] With practice, this can lead you to become calmer and quieter, and this in turn leads to a heightened degree of *kavvanah*—continuous awareness of the intention of everything we do.

To attain this heightened degree of *kavvanah*, Rabbi Cooper recommends contemplative discipline. Here's a summary of one such discipline:

1. Sit quietly with your eyes open. Try to be very still, and let yourself think about a small movement, such as turning the page of a book.
2. Be conscious of wanting to do something but not doing it. Be aware of what you must do before you do it. What must happen in order to get your body to do what you want it to? Next, allow yourself to reach out and turn the page.
3. As you move your hand, try to observe your own act of will to do what you are doing.
4. Imagine that everything in existence is related to a source of energy. If the connection between anything and that source of power were broken, that thing would cease to exist. Imagining the presence of this source of energy, power, or life, repeat steps 1 through 3.
5. Once you are ready to do so, become aware of everything around you, keeping in mind that

the source of everything's existence is always
present. This source of life sparks everything
that is, every motion, every sound, every word,
every thought. Be aware of this as the presence
of the Divine Mystery, or God.

6. Set a timer, perhaps on a wristwatch, to alert you
every couple of hours. Each time the alarm goes
off, become aware of the presence of the Divine
Mystery for as long as it is possible to do so.
After a time, doing this will become second nature. "A major aspect of the enlightening process
is bringing the presence of the Divine into as
many moments of your life as possible."[31]

One important value of this contemplative exercise is
that it helps overcome the difference between contemplative prayer time and the rest of the day. If awareness
of the Divine Mystery, or God, happens frequently
throughout the day, there is not such a big psychological
leap or shift that needs to happen when it is time for contemplative prayer. This means, in turn, that the cultivation of inner silence and solitude takes less effort, less
energy.

Contemporary Buddhist master Osho recommends
a contemplative discipline that attunes us to silence by
listening to a simple sound:

> Go to a temple. A bell is there or a gong. Take
> the bell in your hand and wait. First become
> totally alert. The sound is going to be there and
> you are not to miss the beginning. First be-
> come totally alert, as if your life depends on
> this, as if someone is going to kill you this very
> moment and you will be awake. Be alert—as if

this is going to be your death. And if there is
thought, wait, because thought is sleepiness.
With thought you cannot be alert. When you
are alert there is no thought.[32]

Osho continues, instructing the disciple to wait until his
or her mind is free from thoughts. Then, become aware
of the fact that there is no sound present. Next, strike the
bell and be completely aware of the sound, and follow it
with total awareness as it becomes more and more subtle, until finally the sound is no longer there. After having done this exercise with an external sound, like a bell
ringing, next try it with an internal sound.

Close your eyes and speak the sound of any letter of
the alphabet silently, and do the same experiment with
the silent sound of that letter as you did with the sound
of the bell. "It is difficult; that is why we do it outwardly
first. When you can do it outwardly, then you will be
able to do it inwardly."[33] Wait for the moment when the
mind is empty, then speak the sound of the letter in your
mind. "Feel it, move with it, go with it, until it disappears completely."[34] It may take a few months before
you can do this, but while practicing this silent contemplative exercise you will become more and more alert,
more able to "watch" the pre-sound and after-sound silence. "Once you become so alert that you can watch the
beginning and the end of a sound, through this process
you will have become a totally different person."[35]

Silence and solitude are important to authentic,
living prayer. Without them you will discover neither
the true self nor God. In silence and solitude we discover
that this union between self and God is already an accomplished fact. In the words of a contemporary
Catholic theologian:

You will never find God by looking for proofs that God exists. In fact, you will never find God by looking outside yourself. You will only find God within. It will only be when you have come to experience God in your own heart and let God into the corridors of your heart (or rather found God there) that you will be able to "know" that there is indeed a God and that you are not separate from God.[36]

Chapter 5

Living with Rites and Rituals, Symbols and Signs

Virtually every religion, to one degree or another, uses rites and rituals, symbols and signs, to express and nourish the spirit of prayer. While these vary from one religious tradition to another and one culture to another, their purpose is similar: to assist the believer as he or she strives to live in the world in ways that acknowledge the reality of the Divine Mystery, regardless of how that Mystery is understood. Rites and rituals, symbols and signs, help us to be prayerful people every day.

Because we live in the world, we need visible realities to help us relate to invisible realties. This is the reason Torah and Talmud, as well as many signs, symbols, and rituals, are so important to Judaism. This is why scripture, tradition, sacraments, and sacred art are so important to Roman Catholicism and Eastern

Orthodoxy. This is why the Bible is so basic to Protestantism, why the Qur'an is essential to Islam, why the Upanishads and other sacred texts, as well as countless colorful images of gods and goddesses, are everywhere in Hindu cultures. This is why Buddhists have many images of the Buddha and ornate temples. A Buddhist author writes:

> Truth manifests itself constantly by virtue of appearing as statues, paintings and as Buddhist scriptures written in words, because it's very difficult for human beings to have communion with the Truth itself. Human beings naturally have deep feelings and sensations and we try to make things through which we can experience a deep, compassionate communion with the universe. This is art, Buddhist art, religious art. This is a Buddha statue. The statue is not an idol. This beautiful art is the manifestation of perfect beauty coming from the human heart.[1]

Religious traditions often have sacred places, too, that become sacred symbols. Judaism has the Western Wall in Jerusalem, Islam has Mecca, Catholicism has St. Peter's Basilica in Rome, Buddhism has the Pak Ou caverns in Luang Prabang province in Laos, and Hinduism has the river Ganges. Believers visit such places as a way to nourish prayer and the spirit of prayer.

Since human beings are *embodied* spirits, we find it difficult to relate directly to the invisible divine. Therefore, we get help from religious signs and symbols to cultivate prayer. Even signs and symbols that seem to be relatively unimportant invariably carry considerable meaning, even for people outside a given religious tradition.

> Symbolism is so specific a language among a people that the sense or sentiment of a symbol is perfectly clear to all. Arrows piercing a saint's heart speak of sin and sorrow. A halo *is* holiness, no more need be said. A symbol strikes an immediate equation between two things, what a mathematician calls "one-to-one mapping." Lotus = Buddhism. Star of David = Judaism. Crucifix = Christianity.[2]

The same is true of rites and rituals, actions that often make use of signs and symbols. We need rites and rituals, not to mention more informal devotional customs, to act out and nourish a prayerful spirit. Judaism has numerous rituals throughout the year, and Jews gather weekly in synagogues and temples for Sabbath worship. Catholicism and Orthodoxy are well known for their sometimes complex liturgical rituals and sacraments. Protestants use a wide variety of worship services, and Buddhism and Islam have daily prayer rituals and various special rituals throughout the year.

Some rites and rituals are communal, which means you can't act out the ritual all by yourself. You need to join at least a few fellow believers in order to participate in the ritual. For example, in some movements within Judaism, a minimum of ten Jews is required for a *minyan*, the quorum necessary for communal prayer. Other rituals can be either communal or private, so you may perform these on your own whenever you like. A Muslim may say the daily prayers of Islam alone or with others. A Catholic may pray the Liturgy of the Hours—the collection of scriptural psalms and other prayers chanted in monasteries and recited by clergy and others who wish to do so—together with others or alone. Likewise for the Rosary, the Catholic prayer based mostly on events from the life of Jesus and strung together by a repetitive praying of the angelic salutation, or "Hail Mary."

In all these instances, rituals and symbols function to nourish prayer, to lead to prayer and cultivate the spirit of prayer during times when prayer is not explicit. Because prayer can seem to be an action by which a person or community relates to Nothing, symbols and rituals help function as "go-betweens," as it were, helping people who are embodied spirits relate consciously and honestly to Pure Spirit.

Jews gather together for many of their rituals, even if the gathering consists only of one's family. Passover, for example, which celebrates the Israelites' freedom from slavery in Egypt, is family centered and is celebrated at home. Many other Jewish rituals, such as blessings said for various purposes, are done by individuals. Burning incense and saying prayers in a temple are common private Buddhist rituals. Similar personal rituals are part of Hindu daily life.

We have a propensity to be prayerful not just in the abstract, in theoretical or intellectual ways, but in *bodily* ways that enable us to relate to spiritual realities just as real as things that we know directly through our senses. The signs and symbols, rites and rituals, used by us all express the same basic human impulse to externalize the interior spirit of prayer. No matter which religious tradition we may be rooted in, it is possible to better understand the symbols and rituals of that tradition by becoming more familiar with those of other faiths.

SACRED SPACES

Judaism: Homes and Synagogues

The home is especially important to Jews because it is where so many Jewish rituals take place. One sign of its holiness is the *mezuzah*, a small box containing a parchment scroll. This box is attached to the doorpost of the home, and on the scroll are the words of the *Shema*, the main statement of Jewish faith (Deuteronomy 6:4) and the first two of its blessings: "Hear, O Israel, the Lord our God is one . . ." The purpose of the *mezuzah* is to remind family members that when they enter the home they are entering a space dedicated to God, to a sacred code of ethics, and to the Jewish way of life.

This attitude toward the home highlights the insight that there is something very sacred about the life of the family. Here, above all other places, our most basic values are formed. It is here that we become the persons we are. At the same time, we need a wider community, and this wider community is sacred, too. Hence the importance of the synagogue and temple in Judaism. Both places help Jews cultivate a spirit of prayer in everyday life.

Christianity: Churches and Families

In Christianity, the concept of sacred space is basic to the cultivation of the spirit of prayer for both community and individual. In Christian theology, God dwells among the Christian people. The term *church* refers first of all to the Christian community. In a secondary and derivative sense, *church* refers to the building where believers gather for public worship or private devotional prayer.

No matter how humble or magnificent it may be, a Christian church is meant to be a holy place—in some cases a place of special reverence, even awe—and its specific purpose is to nourish the spirit of prayer. The church itself with its art and decorations is designed to recall for those who view it the mysteries of the Christian faith and to evoke in them a prayerful response. This is evident from the grandest cathedral to the most ordinary local church.

Regardless of denomination, certain parts of a Christian church have remained more or less the same. These include, in most churches, an altar where the ritual called the eucharist, Lord's Supper, or Holy Communion takes place; and the chancel (the space around the altar), the nave (the central part of the church from the entry to the chancel), the pulpit (a form of podium from which sermons are given), and pews (long benches for seating). In many churches, three steps constitute a kind of dividing line between the sanctuary, where the altar is, and the nave, where the congregation gathers. Eastern Orthodox churches have, in addition, a screen, or *iconostasis* ("place of images"), which is decorated with icons. Anglican and Episcopal churches usually have a communion rail, where congregants kneel to receive Holy Communion.

The prominence of church buildings and church architecture in Christianity reflect that religion's emphasis on communal prayer and devotion. Indeed, for Christians all prayer—including prayer in solitude—is communal, even if only in spirit, and the person who is praying does so in union with the entire community of faith.

Stained-glass windows were first installed in the Romanesque and Gothic cathedrals of western Europe. When sunlight passed through the colored glass, it filled the inside of the church with both light and color. These windows traditionally depict events from the Bible or saintly figures. In modern times, they may be more geometrical and abstract in design. Regardless, the purpose of stained-glass windows is to give the interior of the church a unique "feel." They add to the sense that this is a special, a holy place set aside to nourish the spirit of prayer and the spirituality of the community gathered for worship. Abbot Suger, a twelfth-century French church official, said that stained-glass windows illustrated the nature of the great mystery of Christ's birth, since the light entered through them and was changed in a glorious way without breaking the glass.[3]

Since the Roman Catholic Church's Second Vatican Council in the mid-1960s, there has been some movement among Catholics toward recovering the ancient Christian recognition of the sacredness of the family and home, somewhat in the way that Judaism does. While there are no major Christian rituals that happen in the home, Catholicism does teach that the family is *ekklesia* ("church"). This means that the family is the smallest form of authentic church community and the most basic building block of the local parish and of the Church as a whole.[4] It also means that in Catholicism, the home should be a place of prayer in the midst of everyday life, and it is a sacred space, although not in precisely the same way that Judaism understands this idea.

Christian sacred spaces are notable for their emphasis on functionality: all Christian churches are clearly designed for communal worship and only in a very secondary sense—especially for Catholics and Orthodox—

for private devotional purposes. This highlights the human spiritual insight concerning the importance of relating to the Divine Mystery as a community, not only as an individual.

Islam: The Ka'ba and Mosques

The holiest space in Islam is the Ka'ba, which is in Mecca. This is the central shrine for all of Islam. While the entire city of Mecca is considered to be a holy sanctuary, and non-Muslims are forbidden there, the Qur'an refers to the Ka'ba as the "House of God."[5]

The Ka'ba is a huge cube-shaped structure, which Islamic tradition teaches was built by Abraham. Still later, it was rebuilt and purified by Muhammad, who obliterated the idols of what Islam calls the *Jahiliyya*, the pre-Islamic "Age of Corruption."[6] During the five times of daily prayer, Muslims face toward Mecca and the Ka'ba. Also, at the high point of the great annual Muslim pilgrimage, the *hajj*, Muslims walk around this shrine three times. In one corner of the Ka'ba is a black stone, which may be a meteorite and which Muslims believe to be "a physical symbol of the primordial bond joining God to humankind."[7] Both the Ka'ba and the pilgrimage are, for Muslims, means to cultivate prayer and the spirit of prayer.

The local sacred space for most Muslims is the mosque (in Arabic, *masjid*, "place of prostration").[8] While all mosques are built according to the same basic plan, most include features that reflect the particular mosque's historical and cultural setting. The most important part of a mosque is the *mihrab*, or prayer niche. Usually the most beautifully decorated part of the mosque, the *mihrab* is designed to orient the worshiper toward Mecca, the holiest site in the Islamic tradition. As a sacred space, the mosque's primary purpose is to nurture prayer in the lives of worshipers.

Other important parts of a mosque include the *minaret*, or tower, which was originally a separate structure. The *minaret* is the place from which the call to prayer is made. In some cases, even when a mosque has a *minaret*, the call to prayer is made from the roof of the mosque.

Mosques frequently have a fountain to hold the water used by Muslims for cleansing before each of the five times for daily prayer. A mosque also usually has a *dikka*, a raised platform on which stands a pulpit, or *minbar*, used by the *imam* to deliver the Friday sermon. Once again, all these incidentals of Muslim life and worship exist in order to help Muslims be prayerful people.

Often thought of as an extension of the mosque is the *madrasa* ("religious college").[9] This is the place where formal studies take place, and also prayer and worship. The mosque and *madrasa* are not, of course, the only places where Muslims pray. The bottom line for Islam is that wherever a Muslim prays is a holy place.

One of the most important Muslim spiritual insights is the perception that one need not be in a mosque or *madrasa* in order to pray. Formal prayer that is clearly noticeable to anyone who happens to be around is taken for granted by Islam. Thus, prayer is not a merely private matter, and religion is not a kind of private hobby. Rather, in Islam prayer is essential to a way of life.

Hinduism: The Holy Is Everywhere

The concept of sacred place is basic to the Hindu understanding of prayer. According to some Hindu sacred
texts, all of India is a sacred land because this is "the
place where the actions that form the basis of *karma* come
to fulfillment."[10] More localized holy places, however,
include temples, rivers, towns, mountains, and home
shrines. Temples such as the Lakshmi Narayan temple in
New Delhi and the Tirumala-Tirupati temple complex in
Andhra Pradesh are dedicated to deities: Vishnu, Lakshmi, and others. The exteriors of such temples are often
brightly colored and built with many towers to represent
the cosmic mountains where the gods and goddesses
live. We find this sort of phenomenon wherever religion
and culture are one, in societies where prayer is not an
isolated or private activity but is integrated into everyday life.

Countless devout Hindus visit sacred towns, worship in temples, bathe regularly in holy rivers and
climb sacred mountains in order to pray. Indeed, the
country of India came to be considered a sacred place
by many Hindus about two thousand years ago. As
time passed, the concept of the holy place enlarged to
include the entire subcontinent. In the late nineteenth
century, India began to be personified as a divine
mother figure. Hindu songs celebrate "Mother India"
(in Hindi, *Bharata Mata*).

Today, India is covered with holy sites. Many of
them are famous temples of Vishnu or Devi, but many
towns, villages, and other places are also believed to be
sacred. Hindus believe the Ganges, Yamuna, Kaveri, and
Narmada Rivers to be so holy that simply bathing in
them obliterates all sins. Places where two such rivers

come together are thought to be especially holy places where prayer is particularly appropriate and fervent.

Dozens of holy places are located near mountains or caves, where Hindu gods are said to reside. Shiva, for example, lives on Mount Kailasa in the Himalayas, and every temple dedicated to Shiva represents this sacred place. The shrine in the very center of a Hindu temple is usually a place with no windows. This represents the sacred caves that were the earliest Hindu places for worship. Such symbolism naturally leads to prayer.

Local temples or other holy places are sacred sites that have been gathering places for Hindu families for many generations. But the Hindu home is also considered to be sacred. "At all times, Hindus can also worship at home, where a special area will be designated as the family's domestic worship space."[11] In the home, there is typically an altar, a shelf, a cabinet, sometimes even a whole room filled with colorful images of gods and goddesses that is set apart for worship.

Hinduism sometimes even speaks of the human body itself as a sacred place. In fact, some Hindu traditions reject the idea of temple worship and prefer to revere every human being as the temple of the Supreme Being.

Buddhism: Sites of Peace

In Buddhism, sacred places exist in order to help people adhere more closely to the Buddhist way of compassion and peace. The first Buddhist holy places were all associated with the Buddha himself. According to Buddhist tradition, before the Buddha died, he asked that his body be cremated and the ashes placed in several *stupas*, or funerary mounds. These would then serve as places of worship and meditation. Worshipers give homage to the Buddha in much the same way as a Hindu worshiper gives offerings to an image of a Hindu god or goddess: they bring flowers, incense, candles, and the like. A worshiper might also walk devoutly around the *stupa* in prayerful devotion.

The shape of the *stupa* developed in various ways in different cultures. In India, the mound is decorated with depictions of the Buddha and/or illustrations based on various Buddhist sacred texts. In southeast Asia, Buddhist shrines usually are low and round. In Tibet, a Buddhist shrine has a vertically elongated shape. In China, Korea, and Japan, the widely recognized, graceful pagoda design is derived from the parasols that once decorated the top of *stupas* in India.

The sacred space of a Buddhist temple is designed to represent the cosmos. The central dome of a *stupa* represents Mount Meru, the mountain in the Buddhist cosmos that is at the center of the world. The parasols above the *stupa* stand for the levels of heaven where various traditional Indian gods live. The empty space above the parasols represents the highest degrees of meditation attained by the most enlightened of Buddhists. This means that to walk around a temple or *stupa* in ritual fashion is to situate yourself at the center of the cosmos.

Today the temple at Bodh Gaya, where the Buddha attained enlightenment, has been restored. Under the bodhi tree at Bodh Gaya, where the Buddha sat when he became enlightened, is a stone structure believed to be the top of a diamond throne that goes down to the center of the earth. According to legend, all buddhas come to this same throne to attain enlightenment. At the same time, this idea of the sacred seat makes holy the space in which all Buddhists sit to meditate. "Devotees of Zen habitually remind themselves that the spot upon which they sit for meditation is the throne of all the *buddhas* of the past and future."[12]

Some Buddhists believe that any place where the *Dharma* (the "truth" or "law" of human existence) is taught should be respected as a shrine of the Buddha. Some classical Indian Buddhist writings tell of shrines where Buddhist scriptures are displayed with great ceremony as a focal point for worship. Once again, however, holy places in Buddhism are not ends in themselves but a means to a greater end, namely, a deeper spirit of compassion and peace.

Bells, Gongs, and Horns

One of the least noticed but most common ritual objects used in many religious traditions is the bell. Bells of all sizes and shapes are used for basically one purpose: to remind believers of the existence of a sacred or transcendent realm and to call the believer to prayer. Buddhists use bells and gongs to recall monks and others to mindfulness. The ringing bell or sounding gong is meant to get the attention of those within hearing range and say to them, "Remember the sacred, remember prayer, remember the way, remember that there is more going on, more to reality, than what meets the eye."

Some Christian denominations hang large bells in the steeples of their churches. These bells call people to worship and toll on the occasion of a funeral or on more joyous occasions. Sometimes they are rung simply to make music. Catholics traditionally ring little hand bells at particularly sacred liturgical moments, although this is not as common in Catholic churches as it once was. Any religious tradition that wants to communicate something of mysticism and the transcendent uses bells.

On Rosh Hashanah, the beginning of the Jewish New Year, and Yom Kippur, the Day of Atonement, Jews blow the shofar, a primitive horn fashioned from a ram's horn. The shofar, like bells in other religions, calls Jews to a spiritual awakening.

SAINTS AND OTHER IMPORTANT PERSONS

Neither Jews nor Muslims pray to saints because they have such deep regard for the one God as the only appropriate object of human worship. For Judaism and Islam, to pray to deceased holy persons in any way would be idolatry.

For Roman Catholic and Orthodox Christians—but rarely, if ever, for Protestants—saints are holy men and women who now dwell in eternity with God but may still pray for those on earth. Therefore, the Catholic and Orthodox traditions hold that one may pray to saints not as if they were deities, but in the sense that one may ask them to pray for or intercede with God on one's behalf.

Some Buddhists believe in praying to the Buddha or other highly regarded *bodhisattvas* of the past, but only in the sense that one may honor the holy one. There is no similarity in Buddhism to the Catholic and Orthodox tradition of praying to saints.

Although some religious traditions are less

demonstrative about it than others, all religions honor holy men and women from past centuries in one way or another. From saints and other holy figures, members of various religious traditions learn about religious devotion and are inspired to be more prayerful.

Judaism: Moses

Judaism honors many figures from the past but does not pray to them or venerate them in the context of devotional rituals, because they are not considered saintly or sacred. Such people are inspirational figures only, but through their example, and sometimes their writings, they continue to nourish prayer in the hearts of believers.

Jews look to Moses as the one who gave them the law and as the first prophet. Moses is the greatest figure in the Pentateuch, or Torah—the first five books of the Hebrew Bible. God chose Moses as the person to liberate the people of Israel from slavery in Egypt and lead them through the desert to the promised land. "Thus, Moses is the key foundational figure of Judaism and the archetypal Jew," explains Jewish scholar Carl S. Ehrlich. "He is the only human with whom God communicated face to face and the first and greatest of the prophets. . . . He also serves as the ideal of the compassionate leader."[13]

Christianity: Devotion to Saints

In Roman Catholic and Orthodox Christianity, men and women considered to have lived lives of exceptional virtue, or who died a martyr's death, are honored as saints (Latin, *sanctus* or *sancta*, "holy [man, woman]").[14] To revere such an individual includes cherishing his or her memory and striving to imitate his or her virtues, ideals, and prayerfulness. More than that, however, it means relating to the saint as one who continues to live, albeit in full union with God. Devotional prayer with regard to saints includes asking the saint to pray for intentions here on earth, and petitioning for cures and miracles. "Because they reside in heaven in close proximity to God, saints are thought to possess special power to intercede with the Deity on the petitioner's behalf. The veneration of saints involves a reciprocal relationship: the believer declares loyalty and devotion, and the saint offers protection and intercession in return."[15]

Devotion to saints began during the Roman persecutions. From about the fourth century, healings and other miracles were associated with the reverence of saints' remains. By the time of medieval Christianity, devotion to saints was widespread, and written accounts of the saints' lives became popular.

Without question, the most widely venerated and most popular Christian saint is Mary, the mother of Jesus. Devotion to Mary, like devotion to other saints, is based on her ability to intercede for believers with her son. The idea is that Jesus will not refuse his mother's pleas, and there are endless stories of Mary's compassion for those who call on her.

In Protestant Christianity, Mary is honored and respected as the mother of Jesus, but Protestants do not pray for the saints' intercession, and so they do not pray to Mary. Mary is not venerated by Protestants, and she has no place in Protestant worship. Oddly enough, this was not the case with the original sixteenth-century

Protestant reformers such as Martin Luther and John Calvin, who taught that Mary should be honored by the faithful and that she should be included in Christian worship.[16]

Islam: Muhammad

For Muslims, Muhammad is the most important holy person and teacher of prayer. He is respected as the perfect Muslim and the primary example of how to live an Islamic life. Muslims do not, however, pray to Muhammad. Muhammad's life was described in a series of early Muslim writings, which formed the basis for a vast collection of writings about him that developed in later centuries.

The two main Muslim traditions are the Shi'i and Sunni traditions. The main difference between the two is the Shi'i belief in devotion to divinely inspired people called *imams* ("leaders"), those who lead the daily *salat* (ritual prayer). They are believed to be spiritual descendants of Muhammad. The division between these two traditions is traced to events immediately following the death of Muhammad. Shi'i scholars see each *imam* as a direct descendant of Muhammad, and each one must be the designated heir of the *imam* before him. Devotion to the *imams* is part of the Shi'i Muslim's respect for Muhammad and commitment to a prayerful life.

Hinduism: Holy Teachers

For Hindus, prayer is a part of everyday life, and Hindus honor any holy man or woman who can teach them how to attain a condition of peace in this life and freedom from the cycle of life and death. For many Hindus, the basic religious experience comes through a living teacher. In Hinduism, however, the humanity of those who are revered as teachers is sometimes, after the teacher's death, subsumed into the identity of a god, such as Krishna, who teaches his cousin Arjuna in the Bhagavad Gita. At the same time, there are literally thousands of Hindu ascetics: people believed to be possessed by a deity or spirit—mediums, storytellers, and *sadhus* ("holy men") who receive the veneration of their followers. There are many ways to learn and nurture prayer and the spirit of prayer in everyday life in Hinduism.

Buddhism: Honoring Buddha-nature

Buddhists venerate the Buddha above all, for to be a holy person in Buddhism is to follow the Buddha's example. Consequently, some Buddhists pray in ways meant to honor the Buddha. In the Theravāda school of Buddhism, some of the Buddha's earliest followers are venerated as *bodhisattvas* ("buddhas-to-be"), and Buddhists pray to them. Among them was the Buddha's main disciple, Shariputra, who attained *nirvana* soon after his master. He was known widely for his wisdom and as a teacher of prayer. Another *bodhisattva* was Shariputra's friend Maudgalyayana, who came from a similar background and was reputed to be able to calm the hostile forces of nature and to travel to the highest levels of the Buddhist cosmos. In Chinese Buddhist legends, he became known as Mulian, and it was said that he even traveled to Hell to intercede for his mother.[17]

One of the most astonishing stories of a Buddhist holy man concerns one of the Buddha's followers known as Angulimala, which means "Garland of Fingers." Angulimala is honored as an example of how even the most corrupt person can turn his life around and attain *nirvana*.

According to the story, Angulimala was a mass murderer who made a necklace of his victims' fingers and wore it around his neck. All the same, eventually he became a disciple of the Buddha and evolved into a man of prayer who attained *nirvana*.[18]

In the Mahāyāna school of Buddhism, any person may take a *bodhisattva* vow to pursue buddhahood—which is available to all—for the sake of transforming the world. For these Buddhists, the *bodhisattva* vow is the ultimate expression of a prayerful life.

One important Buddhist teacher today is Thich Nhat Hanh, a Vietnamese monk and spiritual master, who frequently carries this message of the Buddha to Western countries. Of course, the most widely respected living Buddhist holy man is the Fourteenth Dalai Lama, his Holiness, Tenzin Gyatso. While Buddhists venerate holy persons such as these, they don't pray to them.

The Mahāyāna Buddhist tradition also honors *bodhisattvas* who were not monks but lay devotees. Some of the most popular *sutras* (sacred writings) give striking narratives about the lives of lay *bodhisattvas*. One was Vimalakirti, who showed by his life that there is no difference between the life of a Buddhist monk or nun and that of a Buddhist layperson. Both can become persons of deep prayer and meditation.

To Worship Is to Touch Life

One characteristic of prayerful men and women of the past was their dedication to rites and rituals of worship. In each religious tradition, worship—both private and public—is an important component of a life of prayerfulness. The act of worship is the response of the human being to an experience of the Divine Mystery, however this Mystery is named. Like love, worship is often an act of the will that may not have a tremendous degree of emotional support or payoff. Still, we engage in worship in order to acknowledge and express the truth of our place in the world and in the universe, namely, that of finite beings who live each day in the presence of the infinite Mystery.

In Judaism, Christianity, and Islam, this Mystery is the personal Creator who beckons people to union with the divine in love. In Buddhism, this Mystery is the source of the oneness of all things. In Hinduism, the Mystery is the divine, which has many manifestations. In all cases, however, the act of worship is understood to be a duty for those who would acknowledge their true status in the scheme of things—subject to the Creator, Mystery, Divine.

Most often, worship is related to the adoration of "the supreme Being, the unproduced Producer of all that is, from whom all things and all events ultimately come, and to who all things return."[19] This perception of the otherness of God naturally evokes worship. There is a human inclination to acknowledge dependence and gratitude in the presence of "the One on whom all things depend and from whom they derive."[20] Basic to Judaism is the perception that there is one God who has absolute supremacy, majesty, and holiness. Worship in Judaism takes the form of worship services both in the home and in the synagogue. For traditional Jews, every day is a day of worship.

Christianity inherited this sense of God's absolute holiness, but Christians also see Jesus as the incarnate presence of God and offer through him worship to God. "To worship is to experience reality, to touch Life. It is to know, to feel, to experience the resurrected Christ."[21]

For Muslims, daily prayers are an exercise of the discipline of worship. To read or chant the Qur'an, even without understanding what it means, is an act of worship. Indeed, for Muslims—as for Jews and Christians—worship is an obligation. For many Muslims, worship goes beyond obligation to the point where informal prayer and worship become the very atmosphere in which they live their daily lives.

This attitude of worship is also characteristic of life for many Hindus. "Worship is held and sustained in the home (where there is likely to be a small shrine devoted to a particular deity), but it readily flows out into temples and shrines, and into many practices of particular devotion."[22] Hindus believe that Brahman, or God, is manifest in many ways and revealed under many different forms. While it may appear that Hindus worship many gods because of the many images of gods, in fact all point to the one God behind all the images. "An important part of Hindu worship involves bringing the presence of God into the focal object of devotion, whether temple or image."[23] For Hindus, all times and places can be occasions to relate the human to the divine by worship, which is the bridge that connects birth and death.

If anything is to be learned about worship, it may be this: worship makes people more human by opening and connecting them to the Divine Mystery. It also seems evident that in adopting a discipline of worship, one necessarily must turn for resources to established religions. To start from scratch, on one's own, is to reinvent the wheel.

The fact that holy persons, living and from the past, hold an important place in religious traditions suggests that there is a widespread attraction—perhaps even a need—for such holy examples to learn from and follow. Anyone who would take his or her religious tradition seriously, and learn to pray from the heart, is advised to pay close attention to this widespread practice and to learn from the exemplars not only of their own tradition but those of others, as well.

Chapter 6

The Need for Spiritual Disciplines Like Prayer

The word *religion* is from a Latin word meaning "to bind oneself to." So religion is how people "bind" themselves to the Mystery, and vice versa. Protestant author Frederick Buechner states it well:

> The word *religion* points to that area of human experience where one way or another man comes upon Mystery as a summons or pilgrimage; where he senses beyond and beneath the realities of every day a Reality no less real because it can only be hinted at in myths and rituals; where he glimpses a destination that he can never fully know until he reaches it.[1]

At the same time, human beings find that while they are attracted *to* the Mystery, they are also *distracted from* the

Mystery. No matter how appealing prayer, meditation, and religion in general may be, there is always the pull of "the world, the flesh, and the devil," to use an old Christian formula. Something there is in human nature that would rather sleep than remain alert; something that would rather make do with only what the five senses can put us in touch with, and leave invisible realities alone.

This is why, in all the major religious traditions, prayer has a disciplinary character. A religion is not merely a way to relate to the Divine Mystery at our own convenience and when it seems attractive. Religion is a means to transcend the limitations of the self, a way to relate the finite to the infinite. All the major religious traditions have a dual thrust: they comfort the afflicted and afflict the comfortable. Prayer itself has the same twofold purpose: to heal and to nourish growth.

For this reason, religions typically include spiritual disciplines—among which are prayer, silence, and solitude, which we have already discussed—that go hand in hand with a serious dedication to the spiritual life. These disciplines are not optional. They are necessary for anyone who would see religion as more than an esoteric hobby to be picked up or neglected according to the whim of the moment.

The purpose of spiritual disciplines is to cultivate human and spiritual depth in a world that encourages, even celebrates, superficiality. "Superficiality is the curse of our age," said Protestant author Richard J. Foster. "The doctrine of instant satisfaction is a primary spiritual problem. The desperate need today is not for a greater number of intelligent people, or gifted people, but for deep people."[2]

Spiritual disciplines are not for spiritual giants or those who wish to engage in spiritual heroics. Rather, disciplines of the spiritual life are for everyone, including average folks who have families and jobs, bills to pay, mortgages, laundry to do, and a car that needs an oil change. If spiritual disciplines are to have any meaning, they must have meaning in the ordinary lives of ordinary people. We need the spiritual discipline of prayer.

It is also important to understand that spiritual disciplines are not meant to cultivate a grim outlook on life. The word *discipline* comes from the Latin *discere,* "to learn." Thus, spiritual disciplines "should be a source of freedom and joy" since the purpose of spiritual disciplines is "liberation from the stifling slavery of self-interest and fear."[3] Those who understand and practice spiritual disciplines offered by their religious tradition are inclined to be happy people, people whose lives are characterized by joy that is deeper than the passing moment.

The primary requirement for those who would take to heart their religion and its disciplines is, first of all, dissatisfaction with the way things are, with the status quo in oneself, in one's own life, and in the world. Even those who embrace a religion out of joy and gratitude at being alive do so out of a sense that something is still not complete for them. This leads us to the second requirement: to have at least the beginning in one's own heart of a longing for Something More, something beyond what meets the eye. Different religious traditions use different words to describe this Something More, but whatever we name this Mystery, there is the perception that in it we as human beings find our beginning and end, our ultimate source and our ultimate goal. In words from the Hebrew scriptures, "As a deer longs for flowing streams, so my soul longs for you, O God. My soul thirsts for God, for the living God" (Psalm 142:1–2a).

Of course, even those who sense this longing in their own depths make their home in an age of materialism, a time when there is little support for the belief that human beings can be in contact with realities beyond the material world, beyond space and time. Even secularists willing to tolerate "spiritual interests" or a "personal religious preference" insist that such interests or preferences have nothing to do with the "real world." Even those who are convinced of the reality of invisible, transcendent realities find themselves unsure of how to relate to such realities. In Western cultures, spiritual disciplines have been excluded from common human experience for so long that few people have the slightest idea where to begin.

FORGETTING ABOUT GOD IS OUR TRUE SIN

Spiritual disciplines take for granted that human nature is not what it can and should be. Judaism and Christianity insist that human nature is afflicted with a condition called sin. "Indeed, I was born guilty, a sinner when my mother conceived me" (Psalm 51:5). Literally meaning "to miss the mark," sin is the way Judaism communicates its belief that in spite of their high ideals and lofty goals, people do "miss the mark" continually. "Meant to be noble, they are usually something less; meant to be generous, they withhold from others. Created more than

animal, they often sink to being nothing else."[4] The purpose of spiritual disciplines in Judaism, then, is to help
people "hit the mark" more often—ultimately, as a habit-
ual way of life.

When Christianity says that human nature is sinful,
it means a deep woundedness, a "disconnectedness
or estrangement from God"; it is "the heart's mis-
placement; a disalignment of our affections."[5] Self-
centeredness ravages our love for others, but at the same
time we often do not have a naturally good opinion of
ourselves. In Christianity, "the bondage that imprisons
us is attachment to self with the fear and guilt that trail
in its wake."[6] In other words, sin is the result of our
alienation from full communion with the Divine Mystery, and spiritual disciplines like prayer help the person
turn around from the inside out, away from being self-
centered toward being God- and neighbor-centered.

Islam does not speak in terms of sin per se, but it
comes close with the idea of *ghaflah* ("forgetting").
Human beings forget their divine origin and goal, and
this forgetting constantly needs to be overcome. We need
to remember who and what we really are. Thus, there is
a need for spiritual disciplines like daily prayer to help
us remember our relationship with the divine and our
need to surrender to God.

There are more than ninety words in the Qur'an for
offenses against God or against our fellow human beings. This makes it virtually impossible to summarize
the many understandings of "forgetting" in Islam. The
Qur'an offers guidance so that Muslims will know what
kinds of behavior God requires. While early in the history of Islam there were some who insisted that a Muslim who sins separates himself from Islam and no longer

belongs to the community,[7] most Muslims today believe that God is kind and compassionate, and it is always possible to turn over a new leaf.

Since Buddhism does not believe in the existence of an omnipotent God or Creator, it has no concept of sin as an offense against the will of God. Buddhism does, however, see a clear difference between good and evil actions. Buddhists believe that it is impossible to escape the consequences of evil deeds and the retribution that will follow. An evil thought, word, or deed is committed under the influence of the Three Roots of Evil: greed, hatred, or delusion. Good deeds, on the other hand, come from the opposites: generosity, love, and understanding. In Buddhism, everyone is responsible for his or her own ultimate destiny, and everyone has free will to choose between good and evil.[8] A life of prayerful meditation helps to keep us "on the right track."

In Judaism and Christianity, spiritual disciplines are not a matter of exercising human power in order to accomplish God's will. Rather, they are a simple matter of opening ourselves so a loving God can do what needs to be done in us.

In Islam, something similar happens through spiritual disciplines like prayer. Surrender is the work of Allah, but we can open the door to our deepest self so that surrender becomes possible. Ascetic extremes of spiritual discipline have been condemned throughout the history of Islam, just as they have been in Judaism and Christianity.

In contrast, Hinduism has an honored place for ascetic practices because they are viewed as ways to liberate oneself from the cycle of death and rebirth and to ultimately unite with the divine.

As the story of the Buddha's life shows, Buddhism

rejects extreme asceticism, believing instead that spiritual disciplines are never ends in themselves but means to attaining *nirvana*.

A balanced perspective on spiritual disciplines views them as ways to open yourself to the Divine Mystery. They are never meant to be a set of legalistic requirements or a rigid set of laws. Spiritual disciplines like those used in living a prayerful life are meant to be a blessing, if you will, and if they stop being a blessing they lose their effectiveness.

Prayer and solitude have already been discussed in earlier chapters. Here we will focus on the discipline of fasting—in particular, the character of fasting as a form of prayer and of learning to know the divine and to know yourself.

The Discipline of Fasting in Prayer

Fasting—abstaining from food and drink—is one of the most difficult spiritual disciplines for us to understand. In the developed nations, eating is not merely what we do to nourish ourselves physically. We eat for recreational purposes; we eat as a compensation for spiritual and emotional emptiness; we eat when we are worried or fearful, or feel unloved or lonely. Consequently, we find it difficult to understand the spirituality of fasting. In a culture where we habitually live as if there were no God, the idea of abstaining from food for spiritual reasons leaves us puzzled. Yet, dieting—in effect, fasting in order to lose weight—is practically a national hobby. And fasting for nutritional reasons—to "purge the body of

impurities"—is popular in many nutritional philoso-
phies. But mention fasting for spiritual reasons, and you
can be sure that plenty of people will conclude that you
are some sort of "religious wacko."

In truth, fasting as a spiritual discipline is part of
every major religious tradition and can be an important
part of a prayerful life. One reason so many people in
Western cultures don't understand fasting, or dismiss it
as a sign of religious craziness, is that in earlier generations fasting became little more than the observance of a
religious law. Among Roman Catholics, for example,
even today the idea of fasting is viewed as simply a religious law in effect during certain religious seasons of the
year such as Lent. Beyond that, few people understand
the *purpose* of fasting.

Of all spiritual disciplines, fasting is the one perhaps most difficult to understand because it can be explained only in terms of one's belief in and openness to
invisible realities. In an era when vast numbers of people
doubt the existence of these invisible realities, the idea of
fasting is difficult to communicate.

To put it as simply as possible, fasting as a spiritual
discipline is done in order to turn away from self, to dis-
regard the needs of the self in order to be open to being
filled by God or the Divine Mystery, to empty the self
physically in order to be filled spiritually.

Our lives as prayerful people become more obvious
when we fast. On a practical level, there is nothing complicated about fasting, but it is important to have a clear
plan in mind.

For instance, fasting holds a special place in Judaism on two days of the year. The first day of fasting is
Yom Kippur, the Day of Atonement. This is the day on

which Jews focus on individual repentance, on their
need to become better persons. It is based on the words
of God in Leviticus 23:26–32: "The Lord spoke to Moses
saying: . . . the tenth day of this seventh month is the Day
of Atonement: It shall be a holy convocation to you, and
you shall afflict your souls; . . ."[9] Yom Kippur is the culmination of ten days marked by the spirit of penitence that
began with Rosh Hashanah. From just before sundown
the evening before Yom Kippur until just after sundown
on Yom Kippur itself, Jews fast from all food and drink
as a sign of repentance. Non-Jews are often surprised to
learn, however, that the Talmud classifies Yom Kippur as
a happy day, not a sad one.

> Because Yom Kippur is a fast day, one on
> which Jews also are commanded to refrain
> from sexual pleasure and bathing, most people
> regard it as a sad or "heavy" day. But the Tal-
> mud's insistence on classifying it as happy is
> more in keeping with the day's spirit, for Yom
> Kippur is a day of reconciliation between peo-
> ple and God (see Leviticus 16:30) and between
> one person and another. When observed prop-
> erly, it leaves participants with a deep feeling
> of joy and renewal.[10]

The second day of fasting for Jews is the saddest, most
tragic day of the year. This is the Fast of the Ninth of the
month named, on the Hebrew calendar, Av (Tisha B'Av).
This is a day of mourning to commemorate the destruction by the Romans of the First Temple in Jerusalem in
586 B.C.E. By sheer coincidence, this is also the anniver-
sary of the destruction by the Babylonians of the Second
Temple in 70 C.E. "The destruction of the Temple, the

religious center of the people, was not only a religious disaster but also marked the end of the First and Second Jewish Commonwealths, respectively, and the exile of most of the Jewish people from their land."[11]

In the centuries following those two tragic happenings, Tisha B'Av also became identified with other sad Jewish events. On Tisha B'Av in 1492, the decree was issued that expelled all Jews from Spain. The only alternatives to expulsion were death or conversion to Christianity. On Tisha B'Av, Jews also remember that the Temple has yet to be rebuilt. By extension, Jews also grieve on Tisha B'Av for all the many occasions in Israel's history that have been cloaked in suffering and sorrow, events that reached their apex in the Holocaust during World War II, when more than six million men, women, and children were systematically persecuted, tortured, and executed simply because they were Jews.

Tisha B'Av is a day of total fasting, a day when observant Jews eat and drink nothing from just before sundown on the eighth of Av until sundown on the following day. For Judaism, fasting is strictly a way to express mourning and a way to show repentance and a willingness to change. By transcending the self and its appetites, one expresses a willingness to depend on God. "The Biblical commandment to 'afflict your souls' is observed by a complete and total fast, by abstaining from all *eating* and *drinking* for the entire period (approximately twenty-five hours)."[12]

Christianity inherited from Judaism respect for fasting as a spiritual discipline. The Gospels of Matthew and Luke describe Jesus' forty-day fast before he began his public ministry.[13] Jesus also takes for granted that his disciples will fast sometimes, but he admonishes them to do so for the proper reason:

> "And whenever you fast, do not look dismal, like the hypocrites, for they disfigure their faces so as to show others that they are fasting. Truly I tell you, they have received their reward. But when you fast, put oil on your head and wash your face, so that your fasting may be seen not by others but by your Father who is in secret; and your Father who sees in secret will reward you."[14]

Christianity uses fasting as a way to be more open to God and neighbor. To fast is to ignore the demands of the false self and tune into the needs of the true self, to create and nurture a prayerful life. In this sense, Christianity shares Judaism's understanding of fasting as a way to show repentance and a willingness to change for the better.

In recent decades, some Christian spiritual guides have rediscovered an ancient Christian connection between fasting and social justice. An early non-scriptural Christian document called the *Shepherd of Hermas* says:

> In the day on which you fast you will taste nothing but bread and water; and having reckoned up the price of the dishes of that day which you intended to have eaten, you will give it to a widow, or an orphan, or to some person in want, and thus you will exhibit humility of mind, so that one who has received benefit from your humility may fill his own soul.[15]

For St. John Chrysostom, an early Christian theologian, fasting without almsgiving had no spiritual value at all. For St. Augustine of Hippo (fourth century), fasting without giving away what one would have eaten was a form of avarice.[16] Perspectives such as these, while they may seem unbalanced, reveal the inherently social nature of Christian spirituality.

Roman Catholics fast for one hour before receiving Holy Communion. Other than this, there are only two obligatory fast days for Roman Catholics: Ash Wednesday, which begins the penitential season of Lent, and Good Friday, which commemorates the crucifixion and death of Jesus. Neither of these fast days involves total abstention, however, to the point where the "fast" is practically symbolic in nature. Voluntary fasting is strongly recommended, however, especially during Lent.

Several fast days on the Islamic lunar calendar are either commanded by the Qur'an or linked to events in the life of Muhammad. The main time of fasting, however, is the month during which Ramadan is observed. For the full month, Muslims abstain from food, drink, and sexual gratification from dawn until sunset every day. When Ramadan occurs during summertime, this can mean up to eighteen hours of fasting each day. Fasting in this manner for thirty days is meant to interrupt the usual pattern of life and remind the believer to focus more on spiritual realities. "Refraining from ordinary recourse to nature's sustenance reminds one of a greater need that only God can fill."[17]

During Ramadan, Muslims fast not only from good things but also from bad habits. These include complaining, taking "short cuts" in one's work, and criticizing others. Revealing the social nature of Islam, fasting during Ramadan is expected to deepen Muslims' compassion for the poor and the hungry. Muslims also fast to gain a deeper capacity to resist one's lower tendencies and nourish one's relationship with the Creator.

Another spiritual discipline that has fallen into considerable neglect in other religious traditions is very much alive in Islam. This spiritual discipline is making a pilgrimage. The idea of the spiritual discipline of pilgrimage is to remind oneself that life itself is a pilgrimage from one place to another, that we are all on our way to an eternal Home, the culmination of a prayerful life. "Given good health and sufficient means, Muslims are enjoined to visit Mecca at least once in a lifetime during the sacred time of pilgrimage, the *hajj*. Muslims are welcomed to Mecca and Medina any time during the year, but fulfill formally the duty of *hajj* only between the eighth and thirteenth days of the twelfth lunar month."[18]

Of all the major world religions, Buddhism has the greatest suspicion of fasting because the Buddha warned against the extremes of both indulgence and asceticism. All the same, fasting is encouraged for Buddhist monks and nuns for special days such as the anniversaries of the birth and enlightenment of the Buddha. Such fasts begin at midday and end the following morning. Laypeople may observe these fasts to gain spiritual merit.[19]

Hindus include fasting in the observance of many of their festivals, such as the celebration of the birth of Krishna. The idea of celebrating by not taking food is just as common in Hindu cultures as is the idea of celebrating by feasting in other cultures.[20]

In all religions, regardless of the occasion for fasting, its purpose is to focus us instead on spiritual values or goals. To fast is to center one's attention—indeed, one's whole self—on invisible realities, and those who fast often report that the experience has immensely benefited them, both spiritually and physically.

Conclusion

The Constant Prayer of the Heart

Prayer is the cure for many of today's personal and social ills. Of course, this assertion cannot be proven. Only experience, only trying it, will prove that daily prayer is what each of us needs to bring our life into balance, is what society needs to bring people together.

When we actually take our religious tradition to heart and draw upon that tradition as our ultimate source of meaning and purpose, then we cannot help but become prayerful people. All religious traditions encourage us to live from a prayerful heart, and when we become prayerful people, *we* change for the better and *the world* changes for the better.

One of the main points of this book is that prayer is not an esoteric practice or form of behavior reserved for special times and special places. Rather, if our prayer is to be authentic, it must be integrated into our ordinary, everyday lives. Prayer is for here and now, in our homes, while we work, in the midst of our daily schedule— whatever it may include. This, of course, is where we run smack into the wall of a culture that makes no room for the Divine Mystery. The beginnings of a solution to this problem may reveal themselves, however, if we see how utterly bizarre this situation is if we view it from a historical perspective.

It does not take a Renaissance genius to perceive that historically some of the most profound influences on our civilizations have been religious and born of prayer. All that's necessary is to listen to, read, and appreciate the various compositions of Bach, Rumi, and Chagall—to name but three of the most obvious—to see how their art was shaped by cultures not yet cast adrift from their religious moorings. Or peruse our greatest literary works to see how they were shaped by religion and the sacred writings of religion. Or flip through a guidebook for any country in the Far East, the Middle East, or Europe and note the almost endless tour destinations that are sites of spiritual significance. All one need do is read a survey of the history of the world to see the tremendous impact of religion. Yet, today we find ourselves living in literally the first great culture in human history to be divorced from spiritual realities.

A superficial scientific and technological mind-set— a practical atheism—dominates daily life, and virtually everyone takes this for granted. Religion's impact on world history is now only fodder for classroom recitation, and even then it often strikes professors and students as a perplexing embarrassment: How, they think, could our ancestors have been so gullible?

Outside of classrooms, of course, countless souls flounder about, sure that their own experience would not deceive them: there *is* Something More going on, and perhaps our ancestors were not as much in the dark as a secular education would have us believe. Perhaps, just perhaps. . . .

If this book accomplishes nothing else, friend reader, may it crack open for you a larger gap between your own heart and the cultural assumption that prayer is irrelevant, unreal, and of no concern to your everyday life. May this book help set off a series of little spiritual explosions in your prayer life, silent explosions that one after another lead to a more authentic existence rooted in your own spiritual tradition, whatever it may be. Let this book reaffirm for you the wisdom of the ancestors and the wisdom of countless unknown companions, from East and West, when their experience and history tells you that prayer is more likely to put you in touch—and keep you in touch—with reality than all the accumulated, undoubted benefits of a technological, computer-driven culture rolled into one. Let this book help you keep on searching and be patiently persistent until you find the courage and humility to work each day at being open to the Light, at disbelieving all that is superficial, mean, and dark in the world until you find the courage and humility to believe with all your heart that fifteen minutes of contemplative prayer each day is worth the sacrifice of dozens of other activities you might engage in.

Let this book be a small, bright signal so that even now, after you have read it, you place it nearby so it falls under your glance from time to time. Then, when it catches your eye, may it remind you of your need for prayer, for communion with the Divine Mystery in the world, in your heart, in the hearts of those you love, and even in those you do not love. Let it be. Let it be.

Appendix

Five Religious Traditions— A Brief Introduction

Few people living in the modern West have more than passing impressions or vague ideas about religions other than their own—if they have a religious tradition they call their own—and frequently these ideas are mistaken. To help expand our awareness of other faith traditions and the innovators of prayer in these traditions, this appendix offers brief introductions to five major religions: Judaism, Christianity, Islam, Hinduism, and Buddhism.

JUDAISM

Cause the words of the Torah to be sweet in our mouths, Lord our God, and in the mouths of Thy people, the House of Israel, so that we and our offspring and the

offspring of Thy people, the House of Israel, may all
know Thy Name and study Thy Torah. Blessed art Thou
Lord, who teaches the Torah to His people Israel.[1]
                                    —*A Jewish morning prayer*

Some seventeen million people in the world embrace Judaism, one of the oldest major religions and the first to teach that there is one God. "The Jewish people is over three thousand years old," wrote novelist Herman Wouk. "Archaeology has long since verified this startling tradition which our grandfathers took on faith."[2] In fact, some scholars trace Jewish history back as far as *four* thousand years.[3]

Almost every aspect of Judaism relates directly to the Jewish practice of prayer, so it is important to summarize Judaism as a whole, not just its approach to prayer. From Judaism came Christianity and Islam, both of which embrace the Jewish belief in one God and the moral teachings of the Hebrew scriptures, especially the principles of the Ten Commandments. Indeed, Christians accept the Hebrew Bible in its totality and include it in their Bible as the "Old Testament." The fundamental teachings and laws of Judaism are found in the Torah, the first five books of the Hebrew Bible.

The Heart of Judaism

The central teaching of Judaism is belief in the one God who calls human beings to act with justice and mercy. Thus, every religiously observant Jew is required to recite twice each day, morning and evening, the biblical passage known as the *Shema:*

Hear [in Hebrew, "hear" is *Shema*], O Israel, the Lord is our God, the Lord is One. Blessed be the name of his glorious Majesty forever and ever. Love the Lord your God with all your heart, with all your soul, with all your means. And these words which I command you today shall be upon your heart. Teach them diligently to your children, and talk of them when you sit in your house, when you walk on the road, when you lie down and when you rise up. Bind them for a sign upon your hand and for frontlets between your eyes. Write them upon the doorposts of your house and upon your gates.[4]

Judaism teaches that a person serves God when he or she studies the scriptures and practices what they teach, most importantly the teachings about relationships with other people. It also teaches that all people are created in God's image and therefore deserve to be treated honorably, with dignity and respect. In this sense, moral and ethical teachings governing human affairs are more important for Jews than are teachings about God.

At the heart of Judaism is the belief that God made a special agreement, called a covenant, with Abraham, the first ancestor and "founding father" of the Jewish people. According to the scriptures, God promised to bless Abraham and his descendants abundantly if they worshiped him and remained faithful:

I will maintain My covenant between Me and you and your offspring to come as an everlasting covenant throughout the ages, to be God to you and to your offspring to come. I give the land you sojourn in to you and your offspring to come, all the land of Canaan, as an everlasting possession.[5]

Subsequently, God renewed this covenant with Abraham's son, Isaac, and with Isaac's son, Jacob, who was also called Israel. Thus, the descendants of Jacob were called the children of Israel, or the Israelites. Later, God gave the Israelites the Ten Commandments. Essentially, these Commandments boil down to a set of directions about how to have a life worth living.

A People Chosen By God

Jews are sometimes called the Chosen People. This simply means that it was the experience of the Jewish people that God selected them to carry out certain special disciplines and duties, such as establishing a just society and to serve God alone. At the same time, being "chosen" makes the Jewish people especially accountable for their sins and other failures.

This concept of "the chosen people" has a life beyond Judaism. As Herman Wouk points out:

Christianity accepts this view of Jewish destiny and rests on it. An important Christian doctrine . . . is that Jesus broadened his chosen communion to include all those who believed in his divinity and followed his teachings. For this reason an accepted Christian name for the church is "The New Israel."[6]

Unlike Christianity, contemporary Judaism does not proselytize in order to win converts. It does, however, accept people who, by their own free choice, decide to convert to Judaism.

The Coming of the Messiah

Traditionally, Jews believed that God would send a Messiah—the word comes from the Hebrew *mashiach*, "anointed [with oil]"—to redeem them. Jews have never thought of the Messiah as a Divine Being. As Rabbi Hayim Halevy Donin wrote in *To Be a Jew:*

> As God's anointed representative, the Messiah would be a person who would bring about the political and spiritual redemption of the people Israel through the ingathering of the Jews to their ancestral home of Eretz Yisrael and the restoration of Jerusalem to its spiritual glory. He would bring about an era marked by the moral perfection of all mankind and the harmonious coexistence of all peoples free of war, fear, hatred, and intolerance. . . .
>
> Claimants to the Messianic title arose at various times throughout Jewish history. The criterion by which each was judged was: Did he succeed in accomplishing what the Messiah was supposed to accomplish? By this criterion, clearly none qualified. The Messianic era is still ahead of us.[7]

Many Jews look forward with expectation to the coming of the Messiah. Others think instead of a Messianic kingdom. They believe, in other words, in the coming of an era of peace and justice that will arrive through the co-operation of all people and God's help.

The Sacred Writings

Judaism embraces two major sets of sacred documents: the Bible and the Talmud. These constitute the foundation for all of Judaism's beliefs, spirituality, and prayer traditions. The first five books of the Hebrew Bible are the most important of all the Jewish scriptures. These five books—Genesis, Exodus, Leviticus, Numbers, and Deuteronomy—are called the Torah. These scriptures give the basic laws of Judaism and tell the story of the Jewish people up to the death of Moses in the 1200s B.C.E. Traditional Jews believe that God wrote the Torah. The Torah was passed down as oral tradition for many generations before finally being written down about 1000 B.C.E. Indeed, the Oral Torah continues to exist and is "bigger," as it were, than the Written Torah.[8]

When the Written Torah instructs Israel to do something, it may not say *how* to do it. The Oral Torah takes care of that. "For example," writes Rabbi Donin, "the Torah forbids 'work' on the Sabbath. What constitutes 'work'? How shall 'work' be defined for purposes of the Sabbath? Except for several references to such tasks as not gathering wood, kindling fire, cooking and baking, the Written Torah does not say. The Oral Torah does."[9]

Most Jews who are less traditional believe that the Torah is the inspired writing of great men, a record of human attempts to reach out to God. According to this perspective, the Torah is neither eternal nor divine and is therefore subject to human mistakes and shortsightedness. Thus, anyone may be justified in eliminating from observance what seems inappropriate in the present era, as seems appropriate to each new generation.

Traditional Jews believe that the Torah is indeed both divine and eternal and therefore may not be altered for any reason.[10] The scroll upon which the Torah is written is kept in the Holy Ark in every synagogue and temple. The scroll is called, in Hebrew, *Sefer Torah*, which means "a scroll of the Torah." In addition to the Torah, the Hebrew Bible includes books of history and moral teachings, called the Prophets, and eleven other books called the Writings.

The other major collection of sacred writings is the Talmud. This consists of legal and ethical writings collected over the centuries, along with Jewish history and folklore. The Talmud has two major parts: the Mishnah, which consists of laws that Orthodox Jews believe were given by God to Moses and were written down about 200 C.E., and the Gemara, which consists of explanations and interpretations of the Mishnah written between 200 and 500 C.E.

Various Movements within Judaism

Judaism has four major movements: Orthodox, Reform, Conservative, and Reconstructionist. Each represents a wide spectrum of beliefs and practices. Orthodox Jews believe that God revealed the Torah and the Talmud directly to Moses on Mount Sinai. They strictly observe all the traditional Jewish dietary laws and the rules for keeping the Sabbath. Orthodox Jews pray each morning, afternoon, and at sundown. Orthodox men at all times wear a hat or a *yarmulke,* a small skullcap, as a sign of respect for God.

Reform Judaism traces its origins to the early 1800s, when some Jews began to question the traditional teachings about where the Torah and Talmud came from. They concluded from scientific and historical research that the Torah and Talmud are products of human process rather than a revelation direct from God. This meant that the authority of the Torah and Talmud was weakened for Reform Judaism, while the Prophets became a major source of inspiration. Today, Reform Jews often believe that Judaism's moral and ethical teachings constitute the most important part of Judaism. This means that many traditional ritual practices, including those related to the dietary laws and Sabbath observance, no longer have any relevance for them.

Conservative Judaism emerged during the mid-1800s. Like Reform Jews, Conservative Jews downplay some of the traditional rituals of Judaism, but they observe more of the traditional practices than do Reform Jews.

Conservative Judaism also gave birth to Reconstructionism.[11] Founded in the 1930s, Reconstructionism maintains that Judaism encompasses "an entire civilization and not only a religion. At the core of this civilization is a people who have the authority and the responsibility to 'reconstruct' its contents from generation to generation."[12]

In contrast to both Reform and Conservative Judaism, Hasidism, which emerged in the late eighteenth century, is rooted in the mystical rather than the ritual. Hasidism teaches that God is to be found in every dimension of life, not just through the Commandments.

The ideal of the Hasidic Jew is "cleaving to God in joy," with an emphasis on emotion and ecstatic devotion to God.[13]

Originally considered heretical, Hasidic Jews today are virtually indistinguishable from many other traditional Orthodox Jews. There are many Hasidic sects, each centered on its own leader.

While the synagogue or temple is the center of Jewish community life, the family is the heart of the matter. Some of the most basic religious rituals take place not only in the synagogue or temple, but also in the home. Daily prayer, the lighting of the Sabbath candles, and the blessing of the bread and wine at the Sabbath meal, all take place in the home. The Passover Seder, the annual remembrance of God leading the people of Israel out of slavery in Egypt, also occurs in the home.

Jewish leaders include the rabbi, who serves as spiritual leader, teacher, and interpreter of Jewish law. Rabbis give sermons during synagogue or temple services, offer guidance, and act in a general leadership role.

The cantor chants the prayers during worship in the synagogue or temple. The cantor usually has a trained voice and knowledge of Hebrew liturgy and music. In many communities, the cantor also serves as choir director. Synagogue or temple worship services also differ among the branches of Judaism and from one community to another. Orthodox and Conservative synagogues typically have services daily, while many Reform congregations have services only on the Sabbath and holy days. In all Orthodox and some Conservative synagogues, there must be at least ten men present, a *minyan* (quorum), before the worship service may take place. In other synagogues, women may be counted as part of the *minyan*.

Making Time Holy

Holy days and festivals are important to Judaism because they make sacred the ordinary and recall significant historical events in the life of the Jewish people. The most frequent Jewish holy day is the Sabbath, the seventh day of the week, Saturday. It is a holy day of rest, prayer, and reflection. The Sabbath begins at sundown on Friday and concludes at sundown on Saturday. Jews attend Sabbath worship services in their synagogue or temple. This time is also marked by special meals and family gatherings in the home. Traditionally Jews do not work on the Sabbath.

The High Holidays, Rosh Hashanah and Yom Kippur, are the most sacred days of the Jewish year. As with all Jewish holidays, the High Holidays fall on different dates each year in the secular calendar because Jews follow the Hebrew (lunar) calendar. The High Holidays come during Tishri, the first month of the Hebrew calendar, which usually coincides with September or October.

Rosh Hashanah is the Jewish New Year. It begins on the first day of Tishri and lasts two days, although Reform Jews observe the New Year for only one day. Rosh Hashanah celebrates the creation of the world and God's rule over it. Jewish tradition says that people are judged on Rosh Hashanah for their actions during the preceding year. The main symbol of Rosh Hashanah is the shofar, a ram's horn that is sounded during the holiday worship services.

Rosh Hashanah is the beginning of the Ten Days of Penitence, which conclude on Yom Kippur, the Day of Atonement. On this day, Jews fast and reflect on their lives in the previous year and express their hope to live righteously and perform good deeds during the coming year. This day is observed mainly through worship in the synagogue or temple.

Food for Spiritual Health

Traditional Jewish dietary laws come mainly from the books of Leviticus and Deuteronomy. The Hebrew word for these rules is *kashrut*, a variation of the word *kosher*, which means "fit," "proper," or "in accordance with the religious law." Note that the purpose of a kosher diet is not so much to maintain physical health as to maintain spiritual well-being, to make even the act of eating a form of prayer. According to Rabbi Donin,

> Kashrut is a good example of how Judaism raises even the most mundane acts, the most routine activities, into a religious experience. What narrower minds look upon as a picayune concern with trifling kitchen matters is really an example of how Judaism elevates the mere physical satisfaction of one's appetite into a spiritual act by its emphasis on the ever present God and our duty to serve Him at all times.[14]

CHRISTIANITY

> Our Father, who art in heaven, hallowed be thy name.
> Thy kingdom come, thy will be done, on earth as it is in
> heaven. Give us this day our daily bread, and forgive us
> our trespasses as we forgive those who trespass against
> us. And lead us not into temptation, but deliver us from
> evil. Amen.
>
> —*The Lord's Prayer*

The Christian religion is at the same time the most widespread religion in the world with the largest number of
members—almost two billion—and the one characterized by the most variety.[15] Still, most Christians have
more in common than they differ on. It is essential to
have a basic grasp of this common ground in order to
understand Christian prayer and spirituality. As a histo-
rian of religion, Huston Smith, has written:

> From the majestic pontifical High Mass in St.
> Peter's [Basilica in Rome] to the quiet simplic-
> ity of a Quaker meeting; from the intellectual
> sophistication of Saint Thomas Aquinas to the
> moving simplicity of spirituals such as "Lord,
> I want to be a Christian"; from St. Paul's in
> London, the parish Church of Great Britain, to
> Mother Teresa in the slums of Calcutta—all
> this is Christianity.[16]

In fact, this is an understatement. There are hundreds of
interpretations of what it means to be a Christian and
countless forms of Christian prayer and worship. And
within each of the various Christian traditions, there
seem to be endless perspectives on Christian faith.

Like Judaism, the Christian religion is a historical religion, meaning that it is founded not on abstract principles but on actual historical events. The most important of these is the life of Jesus of Nazareth, who, notes Huston Smith, "was born in a stable, was executed as a criminal at age thirty-three, never traveled more than ninety miles from his birthplace, owned nothing, attended no college, marshaled no army, and instead of producing books did his only writing in the sand."[17]

Jesus of Nazareth

Christianity gets its name from the Greek word for Christ, a translation of the Hebrew word *Messiah*, "the Anointed One," which refers to a ruler chosen by God. Christians believe that Jesus of Nazareth, born in first-century Palestine, was the Messiah, or Christ. Most Christians believe the New Testament gospels to be historically factual, telling the story of the life and ministry of Jesus.

At about the age of thirty, Jesus began some three years of teaching throughout Judea. An observant Jew, Jesus taught a new way to fulfill the law of Moses, proclaiming that a new order was about to come about.

Jesus called this new cosmic order, to quote the original Greek of the Gospels, *basileia tou theou*. Typically, this phrase is translated either "kingdom of God" or "reign of God," the latter accurately communicating that the *basileia tou theou* is not a geographical reference. Rather, it refers to the presence of God in all of creation, the entire cosmos. Jesus preached that this reign of God was already present in himself, yet at the same time, still had to be completely fulfilled.

Traveling throughout Judea, Jesus taught crowds of people openly, taught his disciples in private, healed the sick, and performed many miracles. He chose twelve men as a select group of disciples, or apostles—the word means "one who is sent"—but women were also among his wider group of disciples. In the beginning of his ministry, Jesus taught only Jews, but later he included Gentiles, or non-Jews.

According to the Christian gospels, Jesus' teachings and miracles soon resulted in opposition from civil and religious authorities. The civil authorities suspected that he was planning an insurrection against the Roman occupation, and some Jewish religious leaders accused him of being blasphemous and urging people to ignore the law of Moses. The evening before his arrest, Jesus and his closest disciples celebrated the Jewish Passover meal.

One of Jesus' disciples, Judas Iscariot, had secretly plotted with the authorities to have Jesus arrested and tried by Pontius Pilate, the Roman governor. Even though Pilate could find no evidence against Jesus, a crowd demanded that he be executed. Pilate sentenced Jesus to be nailed to a cross, the standard Roman method of execution for serious crimes. After Jesus' death, some of his friends put his body in a cave and closed the entrance with a large stone.

Two days later, some women disciples of Jesus went to the tomb to embalm his body. They discovered that the stone had been removed, and the body of Jesus was not there. At the empty tomb "a young man, dressed in a white robe" (Mark 16:5), "an angel" (Matthew 28:2), or "two men in dazzling clothes" (Luke 24:4) told the women that Jesus was alive.

Over the next few weeks, more of Jesus' friends

saw him and believed that he had been "raised from the dead"—a phrase that refers not to the resuscitation of a corpse, but to a more mysterious and profound transformation—because, most Christians believe, he was not in the same ordinary human condition he had been in before his crucifixion. They concluded that Jesus was indeed the Messiah.

Forty days following his "resurrection"—a term that most Christians believe describes an event beyond the grasp of the human intellect though not of the human heart—the disciples witnessed Jesus' "ascension," according to Christian tradition, his final passage from this world into eternity.

Basic Christian Beliefs

The Christian religion is monotheistic. At the same time, Christianity believes in the doctrine of the Trinity: that in the one God there are three "persons"—Father, Son, and Holy Spirit. How can this be? Early church councils, most notably the fourth-century Council of Nicaea, tried to explain by declaring that the one God is revealed in three "persons," and that Father, Son, and Holy Spirit are "three persons in the same substance."[18]

If that does not seem to offer much clarity, it is not surprising. As an authority on world religions, Liz Flower, comments, "part of the essence of a doctrine such as this is that it *should* be difficult and ungraspable—as God himself is."[19] Official Christian doctrines sometimes seem to offer scientific understanding when, in fact, their purpose has something in common with a Zen *koan*, a question or proposition with no evident solution that, when meditated upon or simply allowed to "be," can facilitate enlightenment, or in Christian terms, revelation.

Most Christians believe that Jesus was divine, the Son of God, but entered into human history in order to manifest God's love to the world and inaugurate the coming of a new cosmic order. Through his "resurrection," Jesus continues to live in human history in and through the communities of his followers.

Christian Worship

Worship and ritual in Christianity are quite varied. Roman Catholic, Orthodox, Anglican, and some Lutheran worship services are liturgical, involving the use of worship manuals, or prayer books, readings from the Bible and a celebration of the eucharist, or Lord's Supper—a ritual re-presentation of Jesus' Last Supper with his disciples the evening before his death by crucifixion. Protestant worship services are, generally speaking, much more focused on the Bible and preaching, with infrequent celebrations of the eucharist, or Lord's Supper, if any at all.

Certain rituals, called sacraments, are central to liturgical Christian churches. These include baptism, confirmation, the eucharist and penance. The central prayer book of Anglican/Episcopal churches is the *Book of Common Prayer,* which defines a sacrament as "an outward and visible sign of an inward spiritual grace."[20] Roman Catholicism, in its *Catechism of the Catholic Church,* defines a sacrament as "efficacious signs of grace, instituted by Christ and entrusted to the Church, by which divine life is dispensed to us."[21] Most Christians who attend liturgical churches believe that—even though they are named and enumerated—sacraments are mysterious channels of God's grace through sacred actions.

Whereas the Roman Catholic, Orthodox, Anglican and other liturgical churches are highly sacramental, in the sixteenth century the Protestant Reformers denied the validity of all but two sacraments: baptism, by which one enters into the faith community and experiences the beginning of spiritual liberation and healing ("salvation"); and eucharist, the ritual celebration of the Lord's Supper.

Christian Holidays and Festivals

Annual holidays and festivals are an important part of the Christian religion. There are many more of these in Roman Catholicism and Orthodox Christianity than there are for Protestants. Roman Catholicism has a liturgical calendar virtually filled with days that celebrate the lives of hundreds of saints who lived in many different centuries, such as St. Paul (first century), St. Francis of Assisi (thirteenth century), St. Teresa of Avila (sixteenth century), and St. Maximilian Kolbe (twentieth century).

Special days that all Christian churches share are Easter, the celebration of the resurrection of Jesus, occurring in March or April, and Christmas, the celebration of Jesus' birth, on December 25. Other important times in the Christian year include the season of Lent, which lasts for forty days before Easter and commemorates both the forty days spent by Jesus in the desert before his public ministry and the forty years the people of Israel wandered in the desert during the Exodus.

All year around, Christianity holds its weekly worship and liturgical services on Sunday, in observance of the resurrection of Christ, which tradition says happened on a Sunday. Seventh-Day Adventists, however, take their cue from the Hebrew Bible and observe the Sabbath from sundown on Friday until sundown on Saturday.

Christian Prayer and Spirituality

Prayer and spirituality take many forms among Christians, but the ideal for all Christians is to see spirituality as inseparable from everyday life. Most Christians believe that God answers prayer, if not right away, then obliquely.

Protestant prayer tends to be more spontaneous, focusing on petitions, intercessions and praises addressed to God, whereas Roman Catholic and Orthodox spiritualities are often more open to mysticism and contemplative forms of prayer, using both direct and indirect means of communication with God. Many ordinary Christians are just beginning to discover the riches of the Christian mystical tradition. This includes Eastern Orthodox works such as the anonymously written *The Way of a Pilgrim* and the *Philokalia*, and the writings of Western mystics such as St. John of the Cross *(The Living Flame of Love)*, St. Teresa of Avila *(Interior Castle)*, and Julian of Norwich *(Revelations of Divine Love)*.

ISLAM

In the Name of Allah the Merciful, the Compassionate:
Praise be to Allah, Creator of the worlds,
The Merciful, the Compassionate,
Ruler of the Day of Judgment.

Thee do we worship, and Thee do we ask for aid.
Guide us in the straight path,
The path of those on whom Thou hast poured forth Thy
      grace.
Not the path of those who have incurred Thy wrath and
      gone astray.[22]

—An Islamic daily prayer

Closely related to Judaism and Christianity, Islam is the third of the three great Semitic religions. Basically, all three share the same fundamental belief in one God. "Even if they appear to differ radically in outward form, the intention behind the scriptures, the rituals and doctrines is essentially the same: that of eventual union with God."[23]

The term *Islam* means "submission to God," or, more accurately, "the peace that comes when one's life is surrendered to God."[24] Islam insists that the patriarchs and prophets of the Hebrew Scriptures, as well as John the Baptizer—an important precursor of Jesus in all four New Testament Gospels—and Jesus himself, were all "muslim," which means "one who is devoted or faithful to God." Islam teaches that all of them submitted themselves to the truth and to the one God, even though Islam does not accept Christian belief in Jesus as the Messiah and Son of God.

The Origins of Islam

Islam came into existence about six hundred years after the birth of Jesus. Into an Arab world characterized by cultural, social, and religious discord came Muhammad, who was born in the city of Mecca, a prosperous trading center. During his youth and as a young adult,

Muhammad traveled extensively and gained a reputation for being fair, honest, and wise. In the year 610, Muhammad informed those around him that he had received a revelation, and he began preaching the message of the One God to largely hostile audiences.

Muhammad's declaration that there was but One God and one True Path clashed with the traditions of his people, who saw him as a dangerous radical and a threat to their culture.

According to tradition, by 622 Muhammad had made so many enemies that his life was in danger. He and a small group of companions fled to Medina, where the city's leaders were fed up with all the squabbling between various factions and wanted someone to unite the people. This new teacher seemed to have what it would take to do that. Muhammad's escape to Medina is known in Islam as the Hijra, and 622 is given as the official beginning date of Islam.

In Medina, Muhammad wrote down the Qur'an, the central holy book of Islam, and Islam developed into a well-organized and systematized religion. Islam became not only a religion, but an entire way of life that had a profound impact on culture, society, and politics. By the year 630, Muhammad had become "the political leader of most of central and Western Arabia—even Makkah [Mecca] had surrendered eventually."[25] Muhammad died in 632, not long after declaring publicly that his mission was complete.

The Centrality of the Qur'an

The Qur'an is not only the main collection of sacred writings for Islam; it is the heart of Islam itself. Muslims believe that the Qur'an, sometimes written "Koran," was revealed to Muhammad over twenty-three years by means of voices, the first occurring while he was meditating in a cave at Hira, outside the city of Mecca. Initially, Muhammad reported, these voices sounded like the ringing of bells, but gradually they became one voice that identified itself as the voice of the angel Jibra'eel, or Gabriel. Muhammad said that when the voice spoke, the words fell on him as if they had actual mass and weight. Once the words came on Muhammad while he was astride a camel, and the animal tried in vain to bear the additional weight. "By the time the revelation ceased, its belly was pressed against the earth and its legs splayed out."[26]

While Muhammad was in the trancelike states during which he received his revelations, he spoke the words he received in a loud voice, and his disciples wrote down the words. Muslims believe that God preserved the accuracy of the words throughout the entire process.[27]

Muslims also believe that the Qur'an is the culmination of the Hebrew and Christian scriptures. In the Qur'an, Muslims find the ultimate guide to seeing the difference between good and evil, right and wrong behavior, truth and error. The Qur'an gives the essentials of Islamic faith, but it also tells how a Muslim should behave in every imaginable set of circumstances. Since the words of the Qur'an are understood to be directly from God, the Qur'an is read in the original Arabic, and translations are never used in worship. Translations are common, however, and are useful to non-Muslims who want to know more about Islam.

The Five Pillars of Islam

The instructions that Muhammad received at Medina were condensed to form what are known as the Five Pillars of Islam, the five observances every Muslim practices:

1. The *shahada*, or profession of faith: "There is no god but God and Muhammad is his prophet." Muslims repeat these words in their daily prayers, and they are written on public buildings in Islamic countries.

2. *Salat*, or worship: Muslims are to pray five times each day—before sunrise, after midday, late afternoon, at sunset, and during the night. Private prayer at other times is also a part of Islamic life. On Fridays, Muslims are expected to say the after-midday prayer together in the mosque.

3. *Sawm*, or fasting: Ramadan, the ninth Muslim month, is a month of fasting. Adult Muslims are to refrain from eating, drinking, smoking, and sex from dawn to sunset. The purpose of fasting is to cleanse the body to be filled by the spirit of piety and righteousness. It is also a time to take stock of one's life and be reflective.

4. The *zakat*, or tithe: the right a Muslim community has to all the surplus wealth of every individual. It is often calculated at an annual rate of 2½ percent and is distributed among the needy. Many Muslims give far more than this by way of private donations.

5. *Hajj*, or pilgrimage: all Muslims who can afford to do so, who are physically capable of doing so, and for whom the journey would not be a hardship for their family are to make the pilgrimage

to Mecca during the pilgrimage month of *Dhu-l-Hijja* at least once in their lifetime.

On Fridays, all Muslim men are expected to gather at a mosque for the after-midday prayer. Women may attend prayers in a mosque, but this is not required, and they must sit in a separate area, often at a gallery upstairs. This is not the equivalent of the Jewish or Christian Sabbath because Friday is in all other ways the same as every other day. Also, the mosque is not a consecrated or an especially holy building. Islam teaches that the whole world is a mosque because Muslims may pray to God wherever they may be. The mosque is simply a building that makes a convenient place for a Muslim community to gather. It is not unusual, in fact, for travelers to use a mosque as a place to sleep and spend the night.

Islamic Rituals

Every effort is made to make sure that the first sound an infant hears is the call to prayer. This call is whispered in each ear as soon as possible after birth. Boys are circumcised, but the age when this is done varies between seven days and twelve years.

For Muslims, marriage, parenthood, and family life constitute a sacred commission from God. Parents choose a spouse for their children, and marriage is seen not as an arrangement between two individuals but as a joining of two families. The Qur'an says, however, that the young woman must give her consent; she cannot be forced to marry. Islam does not view marriage as a religious rite, even though an *imam* frequently presides at weddings. Divorce is permitted but is strongly discouraged. As

Muhammad said: "Marry and do not divorce, for the throne of Allah is shaken when divorce happens."[28]

Other aspects of daily life in Islam include education, on which Islam places a high value as a lifelong activity. Muslim dietary guidelines, which are called Halal, dictate that any meat to be eaten must be slaughtered in a certain way, similar to the kosher laws of Judaism. Like Jews, Muslims also do not eat pork, and the Qur'an forbids the consumption of alcohol.

The Qur'an also forbids usury and the charging of interest while encouraging trade and making a fair profit. In modern times, many Muslims have abandoned this traditional ban on usury. In many countries, however, Muslims have established their own non–interest-based banking facilities. Any wealth a Muslim gains is to be used first to support the family. Any excess should be given to those in need. The Qur'an does not allow gambling because gambling encourages putting one's trust in luck rather than in God's providence and one's own honest labor.

Islam teaches that each person's death is predetermined by God, so death is nothing to fear. When someone dies, the body is ritually washed, wrapped in a white shroud, and buried as soon as possible. Because Islam teaches that there will be a literal bodily resurrection on the Day of Judgment, cremation is not allowed. Mourning is expected, but too much grief is deemed inappropriate because someone who dies as a good Muslim is presumed to be in Paradise.

Islamic Festivals

Islamic festivals and celebrations are few, and some months have no festivities at all. The Islamic calendar is completely lunar and is not adjusted to stay in tune with the solar year, as are most other lunar calendars. Muslims count the years beginning with the move of Muhammad to Medina in 622. This means, for example, that the year 2000 is 1420/1421 on the Islamic calendar.

The tenth day of the first month, *Muharram*, is the festival of *Ashura*. The Islamic theme for this festival is the Israelites' escape from Egypt. Muslims also celebrate this day as the day that Noah's ark struck dry land. For two days before *Ashura*, Muslims fast.

As discussed above, Ramadan, the ninth month, is a time of fasting during which Muslims celebrate the month in which the Qur'an was given to Muhammad.

The Night of Power celebrates the actual night Muhammad received, from an angel in the form of a man, his commission as the Prophet.[29] Since no one knows which of the last ten nights of Ramadan this happened on, many Muslims stay in a mosque for the last ten nights to make sure that they are praying during the actual Night of Power, which is usually thought to be about the 27th of Ramadan.

The festival of *Eid ul-Fitr* celebrates the end of the fasting of Ramadan. It begins with the sighting of the new moon. Muslim congregations gather for prayers, and special foods are prepared for feasting. Muslims often purchase new clothes for this festival, and they may exchange gifts.

The festival of *Dhu-l-Hijja* takes place at the time of the pilgrimage events in and around Mecca. In 1996, for example, it lasted from about the middle of April until the middle of May. The pilgrimage, or *Hajj*, begins at Mina, a small uninhabited village where pilgrims gather for the night. Later, they throw rocks and pebbles at stone pillars that represent Satan and temptation. Each pilgrim circles the Ka'ba—the house of worship in Mecca that Muslims believe was built by Abraham and his son Ishmael—touching or kissing the black stone in the wall of the Ka'ba.

Pilgrims also drink from the well that Muslims identify as the one God provided in the desert for Abraham's companion Hagar and her child Ishmael. When Hagar feared that she and her child would die of thirst, she ran back and forth between two hills looking for water. Muslim pilgrims commemorate this by running between two hills named *al-Safa* and *al-Marwa*. Finally, they gather at the Mount of Mercy, where they listen to a sermon that commemorates the Farewell Sermon of Muhammad.

Eid-ul Adha is celebrated on the tenth of *Dhu-l-Hijja*, in early April to recall the willingness of Abraham to sacrifice his son when God commanded him to do so. According to Islam, after God sent an angel to restrain Abraham from sacrificing his son Ishmael, he sacrificed a goat instead; therefore, the sacrifice of a lamb or goat is a central part of this festival.[30]

The final Islamic celebration is the birthday of the prophet Muhammad. Celebration of this event takes place on the eve of the twelfth of *Rabiul-Awwal*, the third month on the Muslim lunar calendar.

Islamic Prayer and Spirituality

Prayer and spirituality are fundamental to Islam. Prayer is not reserved for the privacy of one's own home or for the mosque. Rather, prayer is part of daily activities. In everyday life Islam identifies five kinds of human activities: some are forbidden; others are disapproved of but not forbidden; still others are neutral. A fourth category is activities that are good and rewarded by God. Finally, some activities are completely obligatory.[31] Prayer frames a Muslim life in all aspects.

HINDUISM

> O Lord, forgive three sins that are due to my human
>   limitations:
> Thou art everywhere, but I worship you here;
> Thou are without form, but I worship you in these forms;
> Thou needest no praise, yet I offer you these prayers and
>   salutations.
> Lord, forgive three sins that are due to my human
>   limitations.[32]
>
> *—Hindu invocation*

Huston Smith, a widely respected authority on world religions, says that if we take Hinduism as a whole, "its vast literature, its complicated rituals, its sprawling folkways, its opulent art,"[33] and try to distill it into a single affirmation, it would be this: "You can have what you want."[34]

The catch is, of course, what *do* we want? Human beings seek pleasure and try to avoid pain. If pleasure is what you want, Hinduism says, then by all means seek pleasure. Eventually, however, most people realize that pleasure is not all they want from life, for pleasure is not enough to satisfy the whole person.

Hinduism acknowledges that worldly success also is a worthwhile goal and that the satisfactions of worldly success last longer than the satisfactions of pleasure. So seek worldly success to your heart's content. But Hinduism warns that since other people want wealth, fame, and power, you may eventually lose what you have. It also advises that the drive for worldly success is insatiable and that you can never get enough.

The next thing people want is to be of service to others, to the wider community. This is a praiseworthy goal, Hinduism declares, but duty has its limitations, for all that we do passes away.

Hinduism teaches that the person with any depth eventually asks, "Is that all there is?" Hinduism declares that what we want more than anything else is joy, which is the direct opposite of futility, boredom, and frustration. We also desire infinite being and infinite knowledge, which is better than pleasure and worldy success. To achieve this, we can seek a state called *moksha* or *moksa* (liberation), or freedom from the limitations and attachments that keep us from infinite being, consciousness, and bliss. Attaining *moksa* is the goal of Hinduism, as salvation is the goal of Christianity and enlightenment the goal of Buddhism.

Hinduism states that we already have this liberation and freedom latent within us because the deepest level of each person is "a reservoir of being that never dies, is never exhausted, and is unrestricted in consciousness and bliss."[35] This deepest reality of the self is called *Atman*.

The reason people do not live in terms of their

deepest self, Hinduism says, is that it is buried beneath distractions, illusions, and self-centeredness. The main problem of life, in Hinduism, is to clear away impurities so the infinite light of the *Atman* can shine clearly.

Hindus believe that *Atman* is present in all beings, including animals and that every being goes through cycles of birth, death, and rebirth, called *samsara*. The soul's ultimate goal is to break free of this cycle and merge with God, or the Supreme Spirit.

Hindus work toward this liberation by observing the daily duties of Hinduism: the Path of Devotion, the Path of Good Works, or *karma* (Right Actions), the Path of Knowledge, or *jnana*, and the Path of Yoga. These paths are not mutually exclusive, and most Hindus combine elements of all four. The main path for most Hindus, however, is the Path of Devotion. By this path, *moksha* is achieved by means of daily prayer and devotion to the personal deity, Ishvara, who personally represents the Supreme Spirit, Brahman.

Sacred Scriptures

Hinduism has two forms of scripture, basic to its teachings and devotional life. The first are called Sruti, which translates as "heard" or "God-given" (revealed and authoritative). The second are called Smrti, which means "remembered" or "created" (indirect and redacted).

The Sruti are the most important scriptures and include the four books of the Vedas and the Upanisads. The Vedas are the core scriptures for Hindu belief and practice and include ancient psalms of praise, a manual of ritual and prayer used particularly by Hindu priests, and other texts that offer spiritual guidance.

The Upanisads are philosophical-devotional works "on the nature of the soul, the relationships between mind, body and emotions, the different ways of *moksha*, methods of prayer and meditation and advice to students of all persuasions."[36]

Hinduism and Monotheism

Hinduism may seem to be polytheistic, but this is a misperception. The Vedas' thirty-three main deities are, in fact, distinct aspects of the One God. Each aspect of God has a different image and function. Hinduism teaches that because God, or Brahman, has no physical form and no material qualities, it—note the impersonal pronoun—must be represented by different images.

Among Hindus, God has three major aspects: Brahman, the creative aspect; Vishnu, the aspect that preserves; and Shiva, the aspect that both destroys and is fertile and regenerates. Two aspects of God cherished by Hindus are Rama and Krishna, both considered to be incarnations of Vishnu.

Female aspects of God include Sarasvati, goddess of the arts and learning; Laxmi, goddess of good fortune; and Parvati, who has a benign form called Shakti, the Mother Goddess, and a destructive, terrible form called Durga or Kali, who demands blood sacrifices.

There are some minor gods who are still worshiped today, but most of the original thirty-three gods in the Rig Veda have slipped into relative obscurity. Despite all these gods, however, most Hindus insist that they believe in only one God: Brahman.

At the same time, Hindus place considerable emphasis on what may look to non-Hindus like the worship of images. Yet, it is important to understand what actually goes on here:

> Image-worship arose because it was easier for an ordinary person to worship a tangible image representing the divine concept of God. It was supposed to be difficult for the ordinary person to pray to a god without form or quality. But praying to the image is not worship of that particular object, it is an aid to the worship of God through concentrating on the image of that particular Deity.[37]

At least on the psychological level, there seems to be much in common between Hindu image-worship and the use of images to nourish the spiritual life in Roman Catholic and Eastern Orthodox Christianity. Like Christian images such as statues, paintings, and icons, Hindu images are used to help people relate to the Divine Mystery.

Karma, Prayer, and Devotions

Hindu scriptures teach that each person has a physical body, senses, emotions, mind, intelligence, an inner self, and an eternal self or soul. *Karma*, a person's actions and reactions, determines what his or her next life will be. Actions in the present life determine how close one is to *moksa* or final liberation, and salvation, ultimate union with *Brahman*.[38]

Devout Hindus pray as many as five times each day. Prayers are said either at home or in a temple. A Hindu temple is the home of a god (an aspect of

Brahman), and Hindus visit the temple much as they would the home of a friend. They bring gifts, such as flowers, incense, or food. It is not necessary to worship each time they visit a temple, but devotional actions are required, such as bowing. A Hindu priest cares for the image of the god in the temple and is responsible for performing the daily rituals. Those who are in the temple for worship listen to readings from the scriptures, chant, and pray. On special occasions such as religious festivals, devotional hymns, called *bhajans*, are sung.

Hinduism is highly devotional, and prayer and worship are therefore central to the faith. One prayer, the sacred *Gayatri* mantra from the Rig Veda, is particularly important. All devout Hindus are supposed to recite this prayer at sunrise, noon, and sunset: "Om. Oh terrestrial sphere. Oh sphere of space. Oh celestial sphere. Let us contemplate the splendor of the solar spirit, the divine creator. May he guide our minds."[39]

Hindu Rituals and Festivals

In India, funeral rituals are especially important. Cremation, the usual practice, releases the soul so it can depart to heaven. Relatives wash the body, anoint it with incense, wrap it in a cloth, and place it on the funeral pyre. All this is done in an open, outside area. Carrying out the ritual correctly helps the soul find its new body for its next life. While the fire is burning, a priest says prayers, and everyone remains until all the flames are gone. The ashes are then put in the Ganges River so that *karma* will be washed away by the sacred waters.

Various festivals are extremely important to Hinduism, and for the most part they are joyful, communal affirmations of life. The four most important festivals are Raksha Bandhan, Dashera, Diwali, and Holi.

Raksha Bandhan is celebrated in July or August. Women tie with a red cloth a brother, or a male friend as an "adopted" brother. This symbolizes bonds of protection and affection between the two.

Dashera comes in September or October. It comes immediately after the nine-day festival for the Mother Goddess. On this day, Hindus celebrate the triumph of good over evil. Gifts are exchanged, and there are dances and processions. This is also a day for forgiveness, to make up after quarreling, and to celebrate friendship.

Diwali, the most popular of all the Hindu festivals, occurs in October. *Diwali* means "a garland of lights," which refers to the lamps that are placed in rows both inside and outside the houses. Fireworks and festive meals are common ways to celebrate, and gifts are exchanged.

Holi is a springtime festival, and it happens at the same time as the spring harvest. The people burn bonfires and throw red powders or colored water at one another.

Feasting is an important part of most festivals, but fasting is also common. In Hinduism, fasting earns a person much religious merit, for to fast is to focus one's attention beyond this world.

Another important expression of Hinduism is the making of pilgrimages. Hindus have many opportunities to make pilgrimages to various shrines and temples. No place is more sacred for spiritual expression in Hinduism than the Ganges River.

BUDDHISM

By my aspiration as a buddha
May the luster of mindful clarification arise in the darkness of insensate stupidity,
And bring acquisition of nonconceptual pristine cogni-
  tion.[40]

*—from the Prayer of the
Original Buddha*

Buddha means "Awakened" or "Enlightened One." When people asked the man with whom Buddhism began what he was, he replied, "I am awake."[41] This is how Buddhism got its name, and becoming "awake" is the goal of Buddhism, much of which has to do with prayer and meditation.

The Buddha was born about 563 B.C.E. in what is now Nepal. His name at birth was Siddhartha Gautama of the Sakyas. Siddhartha's father was a king, and Siddhartha grew up in relative luxury. At the age of sixteen, Siddhartha married Yasodhara, a princess who lived nearby. Yasodhara gave birth to a son, Rahula.[42] Despite living in the lap of luxury and being the heir to his father's title, Siddhartha became dissatisfied with his life while still in his twenties.

One day, Siddhartha, who had been shielded from contact with sickness, decrepitude, and death, saw for the first time a gray-haired man leaning on a staff, and trembling. That day, Siddhartha learned about old age.

The next day, Siddhartha came upon a man afflicted with disease. Then he saw a dead body. Finally, the sight of a monk carrying a begging bowl taught him about the life of withdrawal from the world.

These experiences led Siddhartha to give up all

hope of finding fulfillment in the physical world. "Life is subject to age and death," he said. "Where is the realm of life in which there is neither age nor death?"[43]

When he was twenty-nine, Siddhartha said good-bye to his sleeping wife and son and spent the next six years seeking enlightenment. He consulted the greatest Hindu masters, from whom he learned much. He joined a group of ascetics. If it was his body that kept him from enlightenment, he would show it who was master. Siddhartha outdid his companions in fasting and other austerities to the point where he became so weak that he lost consciousness. Only by feeding him some rice gruel could his friends keep him from dying.

Siddhartha learned the uselessness of extreme asceticism by finding the middle way between the extremes of asceticism and indulgence. Siddhartha saw that it was important to give the body what it needs to function at its fullest capacity, but no more than that.

Next, Siddhartha began to practice meditation. On an evening of the full moon in May, he sat down under a peepul tree, which has become known as the bodhi tree because *bodhi* means "enlightenment."

For forty-nine days, the Buddha was enraptured, and then he took what he had discovered to the wide world. For some fifty years, the Buddha walked all over India with his earth-shattering message. Each year, he spent nine months in the world followed by three months in meditation. Each day he spent long hours talking with people, but three times each day he returned to meditation. It is easy to see why meditation is at the heart of Buddhist practice.

At the age of eighty, about the year 483 B.C.E., the Buddha died of dysentery. As he lay dying, he said, "All compounded things decay. Work out your own salvation with diligence."[44]

Essential Buddhist Teachings

The teachings of the Buddha became known as the Four Noble Truths and the Eightfold Path. These teachings explain the human condition and how to achieve the ultimate freedom of enlightenment, or *nirvana*. Buddhism does not teach that there is a God, per se, certainly not a personal God. Some scholars of Buddhism suggest, however, that in a certain sense *nirvana* may be the Godhead, which does not include the concept of divine personhood, even as a metaphor.[45]

The Four Noble Truths are these: Suffering exists. There is a reason for suffering. There is a way to end suffering. The way to end suffering is through the Eightfold Path, which may be called the Buddhist way of life.

The Eightfold Path

1. Right Views—knowing and understanding the four Noble Truths.
2. Right Intent—letting go of want and desire, and acting with kindness to avoid hurting anything.
3. Right Speech—telling the truth, speaking kindly and wisely.
4. Right Conduct—not stealing or cheating.
5. Right Livelihood—earning a living that does not cause bloodshed or harm to others.
6. Right Effort—encouraging and developing positive thought in order to keep to the Path.
7. Right Mindfulness—being aware of thoughts

and actions that affect the world now and in the future.

8. Right Concentration—the peaceful state of mind that arises through correct practice of the Eightfold Path.[46]

Sacred Scriptures, Meditation, and Festivals

Buddhist scriptures include writings that tradition attributes to the spoken word of the Buddha himself, and the writings of later sages and teachers.

Modern Buddhists try to follow the Buddha's teachings in everyday life in numerous ways: through their diet, their work, and their meditation, and by making charitable contributions at shrines, temples, and monasteries.

Because the Buddha reached *nirvana* by meditating, meditation is the most important religious practice for most Buddhists.

Search through many books on Buddhism, and you will find hardly any mention of the word *prayer*. This is because Buddhism is "a way of life to be followed, practiced and developed by each individual. It is self-discipline in body, word and mind, self-development and self-purification. It has nothing to do with belief, prayer, worship or ceremony. In that sense, it has nothing which may popularly be called 'religious.'"[47]

Nevertheless, Buddhism does include hymns, rituals, and prayerlike formulas. There is a "Hymn of Praise to the Buddha's Good Qualities," and "The Prayer of Great Power" is said to have been recited by the Buddha himself.[48]

Meditation is at the heart of Buddhism, but

Buddhist meditation does not focus on a personal, loving God in the way that, for example, Christian forms of meditation do. Typically, Buddhist meditation is practiced by sitting in a quiet place, and it may include chanting phrases, verses, or passages from Buddhist scriptures to focus the mind.

Buddhism teaches that all things in this world are in a constant state of flux and are, indeed, little more than illusions. Buddhism also teaches that all pain and suffering are caused by desire and selfishness. Basic to overcoming this state is compassion or unselfish behavior that puts others ahead of oneself. Caring for the natural environment is one way that Buddhist teachings are lived in today's world.

Buddhism celebrates various festivals in the course of a year, including a New Year's festival, the Buddha's birthday celebration, the commemoration of the Buddha's first sermon, and the festival of the Buddha's first missionaries who went out to spread his message.

Notes

Introduction

1. Craig M. Gay, *The Way of the (Modern) World: Or, Why It's Tempting to Live As If God Doesn't Exist* (Grand Rapids, Mich.: Wm. B. Eerdmans Publishing Co., 1998), 2.
2. Frederica Mathewes-Green, "Should You Design Your Own Religion?" *Utne Reader* (August 1998), 48.
3. Thomas Keating, "Should You Design Your Own Religion?" *Utne Reader* (August 1998), 44.
4. John Daido Loori Roshi, "Should You Design Your Own Religion?" *Utne Reader* (August 1998), 44.
5. Sri Swami Satchidananda, "Should You Design Your Own Religion?" *Utne Reader* (August 1998), 48.
6. Huston Smith, *The World's Religions: Our Great Wisdom Traditions* (San Francisco: HarperSanFrancisco, 1991), 2.

Chapter I: Prayer As a Daily Occupation

1. See Stephen L. Carter, *The Culture of Disbelief: How American Law and Politics Trivialize Religious Devotion* (New York: Doubleday, 1993).
2. Gay, 9.
3. Gay, 2.
4. The situation in countries such as the People's Republic of China, and Russia, with a relatively recent history of communist atheism, is another matter. In neither nation has the government been able to completely suppress religion; quite the contrary. Still, these situations are unique and beyond the scope of the present discussion.
5. Quoted in Smith, 237.
6. *Poems of Gerard Manley Hopkins,* third edition, edited by W. H. Gardner (New York and London, Oxford University Press, 1948), 74.
7. Smith, 273.
8. John Renard, *Responses to 101 Questions on Islam* (Mahwah, N.J.: Paulist Press, 1998), 65.
9. Renard, 67.
10. Seyyed Hossein Nasr, editor, *Islamic Spirituality I: Foundations* (New York: Crossroad Publishing Co., 1997), xv.
11. Tony Castle, *The New Book of Christian Quotations* (New York: Crossroad Publishing Co., 1989), 201.
12. *The Way of a Pilgrim,* translated by R. M. French (San Francisco: HarperSanFrancisco, 1952).
13. French, 7.
14. French, 8–9.
15. French, 42.

16. Theophan the Recluse, quoted in *The Art of Prayer: An Orthodox Anthology,* compiled by Igumen Chariton (London: Faber and Faber, 1966), 94.

17. Quoted in Elizabeth Breuilly et al., *Religions of the World* (New York: Transeditions Ltd. and Fernleigh Books, 1997), 118.

18. Quoted in Breuilly et al., 119.

19. See Renard, 71.

20. Quoted in Renard, 72.

21. Thomas à Kempis, *The Imitation of Christ,* translated by Joseph N. Tylenda, S.J. (New York: Vintage Books, 1998), 30.

22. The scriptural translation is that used by Rabbi Hayim Halevy Donin, *To Be a Jew: A Guide to Jewish Observance in Contemporary Life* (New York: Basic Books, 1972, 1991), 49.

23. Donin, 55.

24. Donin, 56.

25. "Decree on the Apostolate of Lay People," n. 2. Austin Flannery, general editor, *Vatican Council II: The Conciliar and Post Conciliar Documents,* New Revised Edition (Northport, N.Y.: Costello Publishing Co., 1992).

26. Smith, 249.

27. Smith, 249.

28. Smith, 251.

29. Adapted from Paul Carus, compiler, *The Gospel of Buddha* (Rockport, Mass.: Oneworld Publications, 1994), 184–186.

30. Donin, 175.

31. Liz Flower, *The Elements of World Religions* (Rockport, Mass.: Element Books, 1997), 75.

32. Richard J. Foster, *Prayer: Finding the Heart's True Home* (San Francisco: HarperSanFrancisco, 1992), 30.
33. Donin, 179.
34. Foster, 33.
35. Smith, 244.
36. Quoted in Flower, 161.
37. Thomas Merton, *Day of a Stranger* (Salt Lake City, Utah: Gibbs M. Smith, Inc., 1981), 41.
38. Thanks to Arthur J. Magida for this anecdote.
39. Quoted in Philip Dunn, *Prayer: Language of the Soul* (New York: Dell Publishing, 1997), 154.

Chapter 2: The Spirit of Prayerfulness and Playfulness

1. Quoted in Robert Ellsberg, *All Saints* (New York: Crossroad Publishing Co., 1997), 359.
2. "If Were a Rich Man," music by Jerry Bock, lyrics by Sheldon Harnick.
3. Cheslyn Jones, et al., editors, *The Study of Spirituality* (New York: Oxford University Press, 1986), 500.
4. Quoted in Jones et al., 509.
5. *Dhammapada*, 183. Quoted in Jones et al., 512.
6. Quoted in Jones et al., 516.
7. Jones et al., 516.
8. Quoted in Jones et al., 517.
9. Sherman Alexie, *The Summer of Black Widows* (Brooklyn, N.Y.: Hanging Loose Press, 1996), 71. Sherman Alexie cautions us against buying into American Indian stereotypes. In talks he has given, Alexie has remarked, for example, that the only time Indians today are "close to the earth" is when they are lying on the ground.

10. Sherman Alexie, *Reservation Blues* (New York: Warner Books, 1996), 62.

11. Brother Lawrence, *The Practice of the Presence of God*, translated by E. M. Blaiklock (Nashville, Tenn.: Thomas Nelson Publishers, 1982), 38.

12. Brother Lawrence, 41.

13. Brother Lawrence, 41.

14. Brother Lawrence, 24.

15. Brother Lawrence, 25.

16. Brother Lawrence, 54.

17. Brother Lawrence, 85.

18. Charles Schulz, *And the Beagles and the Bunnies Shall Lie Down Together: The Theology in PEANUTS* (New York: Holt, Rinehart & Winston, 1984), 49–56.

19. Schulz, 76.

20. Thomas Merton, *New Seeds of Contemplation* (New York: New Directions, 1961), 296–297.

21. G. K. Chesterton, *Orthodoxy* (New York: Doubleday Image Books, 1959; original publication, 1908), 160.

22. See Paul Carus, *The Gospel of Buddha* (Rockport, Mass.: Oneworld Publications, 1994), 202–206.

23. Carus, 204–205.

24. Carus, 205.

25. Carus, 205.

26. Carus, 206.

27. Donin, 62.

28. Smith, 72.

29. Quoted in Smith, 75.

30. Quoted in David W. Fagerberg, *The Size of Chesterton's Catholicism* (Notre Dame, Ind.: University of Notre Dame Press, 1998), 39–40.

31. Carus, 1.

Chapter 3: The Art of Contemplative Prayer

1. Thomas Merton, *New Seeds of Contemplation*, 6.
2. Merton, 8.
3. Merton, 9.
4. See Merton, 10–13.
5. Merton, 15.
6. Taizé, the ecumenical monastic community in France, is the best-known example of a contemplative community founded by Protestant Christians. It was established in the late 1940s, soon after World War II.
7. Aviam Davis, ed., *Meditation from the Heart of Judaism* (Woodstock, Vt.: Jewish Lights Publishing, 1997), 11.
8. James Fadiman and Robert Frager, editors, *Essential Sufism* (San Francisco: HarperSanFrancisco, 1997), 108. The original is italicized in an introductory section.
9. See, e.g., Mark 12:30–31.
10. See, e.g., the First Letter of John 4:16.
11. Edward Collins Vacek, S.J., "The Eclipse of Love for God." *America*, Vol. 18, No. 8 (March 9, 1996), 14.
12. Vacek, 15.
13. See M. Basil Pennington, *Lectio Divina: Renewing the Ancient Practice of Praying the Scriptures* (New York: Crossroad Publishing Co., 1998).
14. Pennington, 90.
15. See Ken Kaisch, Ph.D., *Finding God: A Handbook of Christian Meditation* (Mahwah, N.J.: Paulist Press, 1994).
16. Bhante Y. Wimala, *Lessons of the Lotus: Practical Spiritual Teachings of a Traveling Buddhist Monk* (New York: Bantam Books, 1997), 81.

17. Wimala, 82.

18. Wimala, 85.

19. Wimala, 87.

20. See Flower, 159.

21. Wimala, 107.

22. Timothy Freke, *The Wisdom of the Zen Masters* (Boston: Journey Books, 1998), 39.

23. Freke, 10.

24. Judith Blackstone and Zoran Josipovic, *Zen For Beginners* (New York: Writers and Readers Publishing, Inc., 1986), 72.

25. Blackstone and Josipovic, 74.

26. Blackstone and Josipovic, 74.

27. Blackstone and Josipovic, 76.

28. Freke, 46.

29. The author depends for information about Sufi meditation largely on Llewellyn Vaughan-Lee, *Sufism: The Transformation of the Heart* (Inverness, Calif.: The Golden Sufi Center, 1995).

30. Vaughan-Lee, 1.

31. Vaughan-Lee, 1.

32. Vaughan-Lee, 2.

33. See Vaughan-Lee, 67–68.

34. Vaughan-Lee, 66.

35. See Vaughan-Lee, 68.

36. Vaughan-Lee, 193.

37. Donin, 179.

38. See Daniel C. Matt, *The Essential Kabbalah: The Heart of Jewish Mysticism* (San Francisco: HarperSanFrancisco, 1995), 1.

39. Perle Besserman, *Kabbulah and Jewish Mysticism* (Boston: Shambhala Publications, 1997), 1.

40. Quoted in Matt, 67.

41. Besserman, 30. See also Avram Davis, *The Way of Flame* (Woodstock, VT: Jewish Lights, 1999).
42. Matt, 124.
43. Besserman, 45.
44. Besserman, 46.
45. See Besserman, 13.
46. See Besserman, 31.
47. Besserman, 35.
48. Quoted in Matt, 120.
49. The outline of Jewish meditation is adapted from Besserman, Chapter 7. See also the good information in Avram Davis, editor, *Meditation from the Heart of Judaism* (Woodstock, VT: Jewish Lights, 1999).
50. Besserman, 125–126.
51. Foster, 13.
52. See Introduction, note 5.

Chapter 4: The Importance of Solitude and Silence

1. Thomas Merton, *Thoughts in Solitude* (New York: Farrar, Straus & Giroux, 1958), 13.
2. Merton, *Thoughts in Solitude,* 17.
3. Max Picard, *The World of Silence,* translated by Stanley Godman (South Bend, Ind.: Regnery/Gateway, Inc., 1952), 15.
4. Picard, 17–18.
5. Picard, 20.
6. Picard, 21.
7. Picard, 21.
8. Picard, 23.
9. Picard, 71.
10. Picard, 177.

11. Picard, 198–200.
12. Picard, 227.
13. Picard, 228.
14. Picard, 228.
15. Picard, 229.
16. Picard, 231.
17. Quoted in Picard, 231.
18. Merton, 81.
19. Rebbe Nachman of Breslov, *The Empty Chair: Finding Hope and Joy* (Woodstock, Vt.: Jewish Lights Publishing, 1994), 92.
20. Donin, 81.
21. Larry Rosenberg with David Guy, *Breath by Breath: The Liberating Practice of Insight Meditation* (Boston: Shambhala Publications, Inc., 1998), 183.
22. Geoffrey Parrinder, editor, *The Sayings of the Buddha* (Hopewell, N.J.: The Ecco Press, 1998), 47.
23. Carol Frances Jegen, B.V.M., "Solitude," in Michael Downey, general editor, *The New Dictionary of Catholic Spirituality* (Collegeville, Minn.: The Liturgical Press, 1994), 907.
24. Jegen, 907.
25. Psalm 127:1
26. Rosenberg, 194.
27. Paul Tillich, *The Eternal Now* (New York: Scribner, 1963), 37. The reference is to the twentieth-century English philosopher Alfred North Whitehead.
28. Rabbi David A. Cooper, *God Is a Verb: Kabbalah and the Practice of Mystical Judaism* (New York: Riverhead Books, 1997), 173.
29. Martin Buber, quoted in *Tales of the Hasidim: Early Masters* (San Francisco: HarperSanFrancisco, 1992), 150–169.
30. Cooper, 174.

31. Cooper, 178.
32. Osho, *Meditation: The First and Last Freedom* (New York: St. Martin's Press, 1996), 160.
33. Osho, 160.
34. Osho, 160.
35. Osho, 161.
36. William Shannon, *Silence on Fire: The Prayer of Awareness* (New York: Crossroad Publishing Co., 1993), 99.

Chapter 5: Living with Rites and Rituals, Symbols and Signs

1. Dainin Katagiri, "The Triple Treasure," in Jean Smith, editor, *Radiant Mind: Essential Buddhist Teachings and Texts* (New York: Riverhead Books, 1999), 226.
2. Charles Panati, *Sacred Origins of Profound Things: The Stories Behind the Rites and Rituals of The World's Religions* (New York: Arkana/Penguin Books, 1996), 117.
3. Rosemary Drage Hale, "Christianity," in Coogan, 79.
4. See, for example, the *Catechism of the Catholic Church*, (Washington, D.C.: United States Catholic Conference, Inc. / Libreria Editrice Vaticana, 1994), no. 2204: "The Christian family constitutes a specific revelation and realization of ecclesial communion, and for this reason it can and should be called a *domestic church*."
5. Matthew S. Gordon, "Islam," in Coogan, 112.
6. Gordon, 112.
7. Gordon, 112.

8. Gordon, 112.
9. Gordon, 111.
10. Vasudha Narayanan, "Hinduism," in Coogan, 146.
11. Narayanan, 149.
12. Malcolm David Eckel, *To See the Buddha* (Princeton, N.J.: Princeton University Press, 1993), 189.
13. Erlich, 36.
14. Hale, 70.
15. Hale, 70–71.
16. See Charles Dickson, *A Protestant Pastor Looks at Mary* (Huntington, Ind.: Our Sunday Visitor Books, 1996).
17. Eckel, 182.
18. Eckel, 182.
19. John Bowker, editor, *The Oxford Dictionary of World Religions* (New York: Oxford University Press, 1997), 1045.
20. Bowker, 1045.
21. Foster, 138.
22. Bowker, 1046.
23. Bowker, 1046.

Chapter 6: The Need for Spiritual Disciplines Like Prayer

1. Frederick Buechner, *Wishful Thinking: A Theological A B C* (New York: Harper and Row, 1973), 78.
2. Foster, 1.
3. Foster, 2.
4. Smith, 281.
5. Smith, 344.
6. Smith, 344.
7. Bowker, 902.

8. See Bowker, 903.
9. Quoted in Donin, 246.
10. Rabbi Joseph Telushkin, *Jewish Wisdom: Ethical, Spiritual, and Historical Lessons from the Great Works and Thinkers* (New York: William Morrow and Co., Inc., 1994), 388.
11. Donin, 263.
12. Donin, 248.
13. See Matthew 4:1–4 and Luke 4:1–4.
14. Matthew 6:16–18.
15. Quoted in Joan M. Nuth, "Fasting," in Downey, 391.
16. See Nuth, 391.
17. Renard, 34.
18. Renard, 34.
19. See Bowker, 343.
20. See Bowker, 342.

Appendix

1. Quoted in Donin, 175.
2. Herman Wouk, *This Is My God: The Jewish Way of Life*, Revised Edition (New York: Pocket Books, 1960, 1974), 7.
3. See Flower, 6.
4. Donin, 164. The biblical quotation is Deuteronomy 6:4–9.
5. Genesis 17:7–8. The translation is from Donin, 12.
6. Wouk, 17.
7. Donin, 14.
8. See Donin, 26–27.
9. Donin, 26.
10. See Donin, 25.

11. Flower, 17.
12. Arthur J. Magida and Stuart M. Matlins, editors, *How to Be a Perfect Stranger: A Guide to Etiquette in Other People's Religious Ceremonies*, Vol. 1 (Woodstock, Vt.: Jewish Lights Publishing, 1996), 212.
13. Flower, 17.
14. Donin, 101.
15. See Smith, 317. The number is from the *Encyclopedia Britannica 97 CD-ROM*.
16. Smith, 317.
17. Smith, 318. The reference is to the Gospel of John: "The scribes and the Pharisees brought a woman who had been caught in adultery; and making her stand before all of them, they said to him, 'Teacher, this woman was caught in the very act of committing adultery. Now in the law Moses commanded us to stone such women. Now what do you say?' They said this to test him, so that they might have some charge to bring against him. Jesus bent down and wrote with his finger on the ground. When they kept on questioning him, he straightened up and said to them, 'Let anyone among you who is without sin be the first to throw a stone at her.' And once again he bent down and wrote on the ground. When they heard it, they went away, one by one, beginning with the elders; and Jesus was left alone with the woman standing before him" (8:3–9).
18. See Leo Donald Davis, S.J., *The First Seven Ecumenical Councils (325–787): Their History and Theology* (Wilmington, Del.: Michael Glazier, Inc., 1987), Chapter 2, "Council of Nicaea I, 325."
19. Flower, 24.
20. Flower, 26.

21. *Catechism of the Catholic Church*, no. 1131.
22. Quoted in Smith, 242–243.
23. Flower, 34.
24. Smith, 222.
25. Flower, 36.
26. Smith, 233.
27. Recent years have seen such an increase in scholarly efforts to study the Qur'an and its origins that historical criticism and interpretation of the Qur'an is increasingly common. Many Muslims find such scholarly research on the Qur'an offensive, just as many conservative Christians are offended by similar efforts to study the Bible and the life of Jesus. See Toby Lester, "What is the Koran?" *The Atlantic Monthly*, Vol. 283, No.1 (January 1999).
28. Breuilly et al., 76–77.
29. Smith, 225.
30. See Genesis 22:2–13.
31. Breuilly et al., 80.
32. Quoted in Smith, 34.
33. Smith, 13.
34. Smith, 13.
35. Smith, 21.
36. Flower, 69.
37. Flower, 76.
38. See Flower, 73.
39. Flower, 75.
40. Quoted in Matthew Kapstein, "The Prayer of the Original Buddha," in Donald S. Lopez, Jr., editor, *Buddhism in Practice* (Princeton, N.J.: Princeton University Press, 1995), 87.
41. Smith, 82.

42. The Buddha's biographical information is based on material in Smith, Chapter III.
43. Smith, 84.
44. Smith, 88.
45. See Smith, 114–115.
46. See Breuilly et al., 109.
47. Walpola Rahula, "The Eightfold Path," in Jean Smith, editor, *Radiant Mind: Essential Buddhist Teachings and Texts* (New York: Riverhead Books, 1999), 90–91.
48. See Lopez, 27.

Suggestions for Further Reading

The following is a list of books on prayer and spirituality the reader may wish to consult for further information and inspiration. Books referenced in the endnotes are not included here.

JUDAISM

God Was Not in the Fire, by Daniel Gordis (New York: Simon & Schuster, 1995).

Honey from the Rock: An Easy Introduction to Jewish Mysticism, by Lawrence Kushner (Woodstock, Vt.: Jewish Lights Publishing, 1995.)

Minyan: Ten Principles for Living a Life of Integrity, by Rabbi Rami M. Shapiro (New York: Bell Tower, 1997).

To Pray As a Jew, Revised Edition, by Rabbi Hayim Halevy Donin (New York: Basic Books, 1980).

Roman Catholicism

The Gospel Truth: Living for Real in an Unreal World, by Mitch Finley (New York: Crossroad Publishing Co., 1995).

Thomas Aquinas: Spiritual Master, by Robert Barron (New York: Crossroad Publishing Co., 1996).

Thomas Merton: Spiritual Master—The Essential Writings, edited and with an introduction by Lawrence S. Cunningham (Mahwah, N.J.: Paulist Press, 1992).

Eastern Orthodoxy

Saint Sergius and Russian Spirituality, by P. Kovalevsky (Crestwood, N.Y.: St. Vladimir's Seminary Press, 1996).

A Treasury of Russian Spirituality, edited by G. P. Fedotov (New York: Sheed & Ward, 1948).

Mainline Protestant Christianity

The Clown in the Belfry, by Frederick Buechner (San Francisco: HarperSanFrancisco, 1992).

Dynamics of Faith, by Paul Tillich (New York: HarperCollins, 1957).

Whistling in the Dark, by Frederick Buechner (San Francisco: Harper & Row, 1988).

ISLAM/SUFISM

The Inner Life, by Hazrat Inayat Khan (Boston: Shambhala Publications, 1997).

Seven Doors to Islam: Spirituality and the Religious Life of Muslims, by John Renard (Berkeley: University of California Press, 1996).

The Way of the Sufi, by Idries Shah (New York: Penguin/Arkana, 1990).

HINDUISM

The Brahma Sutra: The Philosophy of Spiritual Life, edited by S. Radhakrishnan, et al. (New York: Harper & Row, 1960).

Hindu Scriptures, edited by R. C. Zaehner (New York: Dutton, 1966).

The Rig Veda: An Anthology, edited by W. D. O'Flaherty (New York: Penguin Books, 1981).

BUDDHISM/ZEN

Everyday Meditation: 365 Meditations on the Buddhist Path, edited by Jean Smith (New York: Riverhead Books, 1997).

The Miracle of Mindfulness: A Manual on Meditation, by Thich Nhat Hanh (Boston: Beacon Press, 1976).

Nothing Special: Living Zen, by Charlotte Joko Beck (San Francisco: HarperSanFrancisco, 1993).

RELIGIOUS TRADITIONS IN DIALOGUE

Christian Mysticism East and West, by Maria Jaoudi (Mahwah, N.J.: Paulist Press, 1998).

Forgotten Truth: The Common Vision of the World's Religions, by Huston Smith (San Francisco: HarperSanFrancisco, 1976, 1992).

The Good Heart: A Buddhist Perspective on the Teachings of Jesus, by His Holiness the Dalai Lama (Boston: Wisdom Publications, 1996).

Mystics and Zen Masters, by Thomas Merton (New York: Simon & Schuster, 1959).

Notes

Notes

Notes

Notes

About SKYLIGHT PATHS Publishing

Through spirituality, our religious beliefs are increasingly becoming *a part of* our lives, rather than *apart from* our lives. Nevertheless, while many people are more interested than ever in spiritual growth, they are less firmly planted in *traditional* religion. To deepen their relationship to the sacred, people want to learn from their own and other faith traditions, in new ways.

SkyLight Paths sees both believers and seekers as a community that increasingly transcends traditional boundaries of religion and denomination. Many people want to learn from each other, *walking together, finding the way.*

The SkyLight Paths staff is made up of people of many faiths. We are a small, highly committed group of people, a reflection of the religious diversity that now exists in most neighborhoods, most families. We will succeed only if our books make a difference in your life.

We at SkyLight Paths take great care to produce beautiful books that present meaningful spiritual content in a form that reflects the art of making high quality books. Therefore, we want to acknowledge those who contributed to the production of this book.

PRODUCTION
Bronwen Battaglia, Bridgett Taylor, David Wall

EDITORIAL & PROOFREADING
Jennifer Goneau & Martha McKinney

COVER ART & DESIGN
Drena Fagen

PRINTING AND BINDING
Lake Book, Melrose Park, Illinois

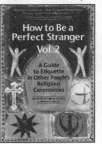

Other Interesting Books—Spirituality

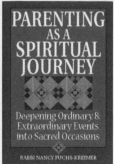

PARENTING AS A SPIRITUAL JOURNEY
Deepening Ordinary & Extraordinary Events into Sacred Occasions
by Rabbi Nancy Fuchs-Kreimer

A perfect gift for the new parent, and a helpful guidebook for those seeking to re-envision family life. Draws on experiences of the author and over 100 parents of many faiths, revealing the transformative spiritual adventure that parents can experience while bringing up their children. Rituals, prayers, and passages from sacred Jewish texts—as well as from other religious traditions—are woven throughout the book.

> "This is really relevant spirituality. I love her book."
> —*Sylvia Boorstein, author of* It's Easier Than You Think *and mother of four*

6" x 9", 224 pp. Quality Paperback, ISBN 1-58023-016-4 **$16.95**

THE EMPTY CHAIR: FINDING HOPE & JOY
Timeless Wisdom from a Hasidic Master, Rebbe Nachman of Breslov
Adapted by Moshe Mykoff and the Breslov Research Institute

A "little treasure" of aphorisms and advice for living joyously and spiritually today, written 200 years ago, but startlingly fresh in meaning and use. Challenges and helps us to move from stress and sadness to hope and joy.

Teacher, guide and spiritual master Rebbe Nachman provides vital words of inspiration and wisdom for life today for people of any faith, or of no faith.

> "For anyone of any faith, this is a book of healing and wholeness, of being alive!"
> — *Bookviews*

•AWARD WINNER•

4" x 6", 128 pp., 2-color text, Deluxe Paperback, ISBN 1-879045-67-2 **$9.95**

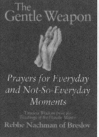

THE GENTLE WEAPON
Prayers for Everyday and Not-So-Everyday Moments
Timeless Wisdom from the Teachings of Rebbe Nachman of Breslov
by Moshe Mykoff and S.C. Mizrahi, together with the Breslov Research Institute

A small treasury of prayers that will open your heart and soul and give voice to your deepest yearnings. A source of comfort for those in search of an uplifting perspective on life, using the warm insights and generous wisdom of Hasidic master Rebbe Nachman of Breslov.

4" x 6", 144 pp., 2-color text, Deluxe Paperback, ISBN 1-58023-022-9 **$9.95**

GOD WHISPERS
Stories of the Soul, Lessons of the Heart
by Karyn D. Kedar

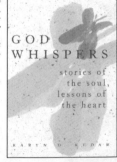

Eloquent stories from the lives of ordinary people teach readers that the joy and pain in our lives have meaning and purpose, and that by fully embracing life's highs and lows, we can enrich our spiritual well-being. Helps us cope with difficulties such as divorce and reconciliation, illness, loss, conflict and forgiveness, loneliness and isolation.

6" x 9", 176 pp. Hardcover, ISBN 1-58023-023-7 **$19.95**

Other Interesting Books—Spirituality

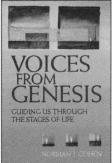

VOICES FROM GENESIS
Guiding Us Through the Stages of Life
by *Norman J. Cohen*

A brilliant blending of modern midrash (finding contemporary meaning from ancient Jewish texts) and the life stages of Erik Erikson's developmental psychology. Shows how the pathways of our lives are quite similar to those of the leading figures of Genesis who speak directly to us, telling of their spiritual and emotional journeys.

6" x 9", 192 pp. HC, ISBN 1-879045-75-3 **$21.95**

SELF, STRUGGLE & CHANGE
Family Conflict Stories in Genesis and Their Healing Insights for Our Lives
by *Norman J. Cohen*

The people described by the biblical writers of Genesis were in situations and relationships very much like our own. We identify with them. Their stories still speak to us because they are about the same problems we deal with every day. Here a modern master of biblical interpretation brings us greater understanding of the ancient text and of ourselves in this intriguing re-telling of conflict between husband and wife, father and son, brothers, and sisters.

6" x 9", 224 pp. Quality Paperback, ISBN 1-879045-66-4 **$16.95**
HC, ISBN -19-2 **$21.95**

FINDING JOY
A Practical Spiritual Guide to Happiness
by *Dannel I. Schwartz* with *Mark Hass*

Searching for happiness in our modern world of stress and struggle is common; *finding* it is more unusual. This guide explores and explains how to find joy through a time-honored, creative—and surprisingly practical—approach based on the teachings of Jewish mysticism and *Kabbalah*.

> "Lovely, simple introduction to Kabbalah....
> A singular contribution."
> —*American Library Association's* Booklist

6" x 9", 192 pp. Quality Paperback, ISBN 1-58023-009-1 **$14.95**
HC, ISBN 1-879045-53-2 **$19.95**

•AWARD WINNER•

MOSES—THE PRINCE, THE PROPHET
His Life, Legend & Message for Our Lives
by *Rabbi Levi Meier, Ph.D.*

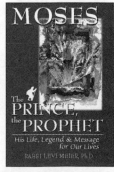

How can the struggles of a great biblical figure teach us to cope with our own lives today? A fascinating portrait of the struggles, failures, and triumphs of Moses, a central figure in Jewish, Christian, and Islamic tradition. Drawing upon stories from Exodus, *midrash* (finding contemporary meaning from ancient Jewish texts), the teachings of Jewish mystics, modern texts, and psychotherapy, Meier offers new ways to create our own path to self-knowledge and self-fulfillment—and face life's difficulties head-on.

6" x 9", 224 pp. Quality Paperback, ISBN 1-58023-069-5 **$16.95**
HC, ISBN -013-X **$23.95**

Children's Spirituality

•AWARD WINNER•

A PRAYER FOR THE EARTH
The Story of Naamah, Noah's Wife
by *Sandy Eisenberg Sasso*   **For ages 4 and up**
Full-color illustrations by *Bethanne Andersen*

NONDENOMINATIONAL, NONSECTARIAN

This new story, based on an ancient text, opens readers' religious imaginations to new ideas about the well-known story of the Flood. When God tells Noah to bring the animals of the world onto the ark, God *also* calls on Naamah, Noah's wife, to save each plant on Earth.

9" x 12", 32 pp. HC, Full-color illus., ISBN 1-879045-60-5 **$16.95**

THE 11TH COMMANDMENT
Wisdom from Our Children
For all ages   by *The Children of America*

MULTICULTURAL, NONDENOMINATIONAL, NONSECTARIAN

"If there were an Eleventh Commandment, what would it be?"
Children of many religious denominations across America answer this question—in their own drawings and words—in *The 11th Commandment*.

8" x 10", 48 pp. HC, Full-color illus., ISBN 1-879045-46-X **$16.95**

•AWARD WINNER•

•AWARD WINNER•

IN OUR IMAGE
God's First Creatures
by *Nancy Sohn Swartz*   **For ages 4 and up**
Full-color illustrations by *Melanie Hall*

NONDENOMINATIONAL, NONSECTARIAN

A playful new twist to the Creation story. Celebrates the inter-connectedness of nature and the harmony of all living things.

9" x 12", 32 pp. HC, Full-color illus., ISBN 1-879045-99-0 **$16.95**

FOR HEAVEN'S SAKE
For ages 4 and up   by *Sandy Eisenberg Sasso*
Full-color illustrations by *Kathryn Kunz Finney*

MULTICULTURAL, NONDENOMINATIONAL, NONSECTARIAN
"For heaven's sake, Isaiah!"

People said "for heaven's sake" to Isaiah a lot. Everyone talked about heaven. "Thank heavens." "Heaven forbid." "For heaven's sake, Isaiah." But no one would say what heaven was or how to find it.

So Isaiah became determined to find out where heaven is. After seeking answers from many different people, he found that heaven wasn't so difficult to find after all.

9" x 12", 32 pp. HC, Full-color illus., ISBN 1-58023-054-7 **$16.95**

Children's Spirituality

•AWARD WINNER•

BUT GOD REMEMBERED
Stories of Women from Creation to the Promised Land

For ages 8 and up

by *Sandy Eisenberg Sasso*
Full-color illustrations by *Bethanne Andersen*

NONDENOMINATIONAL, NONSECTARIAN

A fascinating collection of four different stories of women only briefly mentioned in biblical tradition and religious texts, but never before explored. Award-winning author Sasso brings to life the intriguing stories of Lilith, Serach, Bityah, and the Daughters of Z, courageous and strong women from ancient tradition. All teach important values through their faith and actions.

9" x 12", 32 pp. HC, Full-color illus., ISBN 1-879045-43-5 **$16.95**

IN GOD'S NAME

For ages 4 and up

by *Sandy Eisenberg Sasso*
Full-color illustrations by *Phoebe Stone*

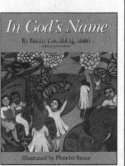

Selected as Outstanding by Parent Council, Ltd.™

MULTICULTURAL, NONDENOMINATIONAL, NONSECTARIAN

Like an ancient myth in its poetic text and vibrant illustrations, this modern fable about the search for God's name celebrates the diversity and, at the same time, the unity of all the people of the world. Each seeker claims he or she alone knows the answer. Finally, they come together and learn what God's name really is, sharing the ultimate harmony of belief in one God by people of all faiths, all backgrounds.

•AWARD WINNER•

9" x 12", 32 pp. HC, Full color illus., ISBN 1-879045-26-5 **$16.95**

GOD IN BETWEEN

For ages 4 and up

by *Sandy Eisenberg Sasso*
Full-color illustrations by *Sally Sweetland*

NONDENOMINATIONAL, NONSECTARIAN, MULTICULTURAL

If you wanted to find God, where would you look?

A magical, mythical tale that teaches that God can be found where we are: within all of us and the relationships between us.

9" x 12", 32 pp. HC, Full-color illus., ISBN 1-879045-86-9 **$16.95**

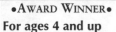

•AWARD WINNER•

For ages 4 and up

GOD'S PAINTBRUSH

by *Sandy Eisenberg Sasso*
Full-color illustrations by *Annette Compton*

MULTICULTURAL, NONDENOMINATIONAL, NONSECTARIAN

Invites children of all faiths and backgrounds to encounter God openly in their own lives. Wonderfully interactive, provides questions adult and child can explore together at the end of each episode.

•AWARD WINNER•

11" x 8½", 32 pp. HC, Full-color illus., ISBN 1-879045-22-2 **$16.95**

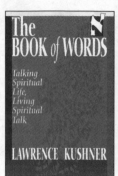

Spiritual Inspiration . . .
The Kushner Series

EYES REMADE FOR WONDER
A Lawrence Kushner Reader
Introduction by *Thomas Moore*, author of *Care of the Soul* and other books

A treasury of insight from one of the most creative spiritual thinkers in America. Whether you are new to Kushner or a devoted fan, his insights will stir your soul. With samplings from each of Kushner's works, and a generous amount of new material, this is a book to be savored, to be read and reread, each time discovering deeper layers of meaning in our lives. Offers something unique to both the spiritual seeker and the committed person of faith.

6" x 9", 240 pp. Quality PB, ISBN 1-58023-042-3 **$16.95**
HC, ISBN -014-8 **$23.95**

GOD WAS IN THIS PLACE & I, i DID NOT KNOW
Finding Self, Spirituality & Ultimate Meaning
by *Lawrence Kushner*

Who am I? Who is God? Kushner creates inspiring interpretations of Jacob's dream in Genesis, opening a window into Jewish spirituality for people of all faiths and backgrounds. In a fascinating blend of scholarship, imagination, psychology and history, seven Jewish spiritual masters ask and answer fundamental questions of human experience.

"Rich and intriguing."
—*M. Scott Peck, M.D.,*
author of The Road Less Traveled

6" x 9", 192 pp. Quality Paperback, ISBN 1-879045-33-8 **$16.95**

HONEY FROM THE ROCK
An Easy Introduction to Jewish Mysticism
by *Lawrence Kushner*

Quite simply the easiest introduction to Jewish mysticism you can read.

An introduction to the ten gates of Jewish mysticism and how they apply to daily life.

6" x 9", 176 pp. Quality Paperback, ISBN 1-879045-02-8 **$14.95**

THE RIVER OF LIGHT
Spirituality, Judaism, Consciousness
by *Lawrence Kushner*

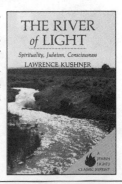

A "manual" for all spiritual travelers who would attempt a spiritual journey in our times. Taking us step by step, Kushner allows us to discover the meaning of our own quest: "to allow the river of light—the deepest currents of consciousness—to rise to the surface and animate our lives."

6" x 9", 192 pp. Quality Paperback, ISBN 1-879045-03-6 **$14.95**

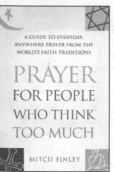